Encountering Jesus

New Evangelisation in Practice

Pat Collins, C.M

New Life Publishing

'Donatus, this is a cheerful world indeed as I see it from my fair garden, under the shadow of my vines. But if I could ascend some high mountain, and look out over the wide lands, you know very well that I should see: brigands on the highways, pirates on the seas, armies fighting, cities burning, in the amphi-theaters men murdered to please applauding crowds, selfishness and cruelty and misery and despair under all roofs. It is a bad world, Donatus, an incredibly bad world. But I have discovered in the midst of it a company of quiet and holy people who have learned a great secret. They have found a joy which is a thousand times better than any of the pleasures of our sinful life. They are despised and persecuted, but they care not: they are masters of their souls. They have overcome the world. These people, Donatus, are the Christians, - and I am one of them.'   *(Letter of St Cyprian to Donatus 249 A.D.)*

'The transmission of the Christian faith consists primarily in proclaiming Jesus Christ in order to lead others to faith in him'
(Catechism of the Catholic Church par. 425).

CONTENTS

Foreword 1

Introduction 5

Section One: Prologue
1. The Need for a New Evangelisation 15
2. Models of Evangelisation 23

Section Two: Evangelisation and New Evangelisation
3. Evangelisation: its Nature and Purpose 35
4. The New Evangelisation Explained 43
5. Conversion as the Aim of Evangelisation 51

Section Three: The Core Message
6. The Good News Message of Jesus Christ 61
7. The Good News Message of St Paul 69
8. The Good News Message in Six Points 77

Section Four: Power for the New Evangelisation
9. The Holy Spirit and the New Evangelisation 87
10. The Gifts of the Spirit and Evangelisation 97
11. The Word of God and Evangelisation 105
12. Community and Evangelisation 113
13. Ecumenism and Evangelisation 121
14. Intercession for Evangelisers 129

Continued...

CONTENTS

...Continued

Section Five: Forms and means of Evangelisation
15. Person-to-person Evangelisation 139
16. Prayer ministry in Evangelisation 147
17. Evangelisation and Deliverance from Evil Spirits 155
18. Families and Evangelisation 163
19. Evangelisation of and by Young Adults 173
20. Evangelising Unbelievers 183
21. Pope Francis on Evangelising the Least, the Last and the Lost 191
22. Holiness, Witness and Evangelisation 201
23. Building a Missionary Diocese 209
24. Conversion of Parish Structures and the New Evangelisation 217
25. The Homily and the New Evangelisation 225
26. Evangelising Courses in the Parish 235
27. Nurturing the Faith of the Evangelised 243

Section Six: Conclusion
28. Prayerful Reflection on Evangelisation 257
29. Some obstacles to Evangelisation 265
30. The Courage to Evangelise: Some personal reflections 275

Foreword

In 2001 Pope John Paul II wrote of the need to *contemplate the face of Christ* - a face of sorrow as well as the face of the One who is Risen - if we are to be disciples in the current age. All evangelisation brings people to see Jesus – and all mission of behalf of the Church has to '*start afresh from Christ*'. As Pope John Paul II put it, 'It is not therefore a matter of inventing a 'new programme'. The programme already exists: it is the plan found in the Gospel and in the living Tradition, it is the same as ever. Ultimately, it has its centre in Christ himself, who is to be known, loved and imitated.' *(Novo Millennio Ineunte 29)*.

A few years later his successor made a similar point. *'Being Christian is not the result of an ethical choice or a lofty idea, but the encounter with an event, a person, which gives life a new horizon and a decisive direction.'* (*Deus Caritas Est* 1) That word 'encounter' appears some 17 times Pope Benedict XVI's first encyclical, where he refers to encountering - face to face - the living God, God's agape, the Eucharistic Lord, Christ, the Father.

And in his Bull of Indiction for the Year of Mercy, Pope Francis would refer to Jesus as '*the face of the Father's mercy*'.

From these great Popes it is quite explicit that encountering God in Christ lies at the heart of the new evangelisation.

We live in a political environment where some look back nostalgically and want to make their country 'great again'. In that context, there is the temptation to look at the new evangelisation as a move to 'make Catholicism great again'. This reveals a deeply flawed understanding of mission in that it risks putting the Church at the centre of the picture rather than Jesus. The Church is there to proclaim Jesus, rather than Jesus being there to make the visible Church feel strong and secure. Our only boast is Jesus Christ and him crucified (Cf 1 Cor 2:2 and Gal 6:14).

Nowadays, we have learned much about how professional communicators get their message across. In the Church, we can learn something from the empirical sciences. But we are not selling a product. We are introducing people to Christ. It is the power of God's grace that attracts, not the mellifluous words that we use. *Cor ad cor loquitur,* as Cardinal Newman put it. We share what we have received and we cannot give what we do not have.

Thus, the best preparation for new evangelisation is not the learning of new techniques but the opening of our hearts to the Lord in prayer. It was while praying that the early Christian community in Antioch sensed the Spirit's call to send Paul and Barnabas on their first missionary journey. (Acts 13:3) The work of the new evangelisation calls believers and non-believers to metanoia. The exodus experience is one that we all have to live. Those who wish to evangelise have to constantly be open to be evangelised.

And in the Catholic tradition, the call to become a disciple of Jesus is an invitation from a community to come into the community of the Pilgrim People. The vertical and horizontal dimensions of discipleship cannot be separated. From the Acts of the Apostles, we see that what attracted people was primarily seeing a group of believers where the encounter with the risen Christ was a lived experience. As Pope Paul VI noted, people listen to teachers when they are witnesses of what they say. In that community of the Incarnate God we encounter in many ways, but specifically in Word and Sacrament, in sacred places and times. When it comes to evangelising, Church is the context for, and inherent to the content of the faith that is handed on.

The call to evangelise thus is not just a question of challenging the people of our day to obey the Gospel. It is also firstly a challenge to believers to know the Lord, to hear the uncomfortable Gospel that we wish to share. Then we have to discover ways to share what we have been given. And finally we need to ensure that our ways of being Church reveal Christ.

This present volume builds on core publications that already exist In the Irish Church. We have clarity about the basic direction in *Share the Good News the National Directory for Catechesis in Ireland* (2010), as well as in *Called Together. Making a Difference. A Framework Document for Youth ministry in Ireland*

(2009). On top of these process documents, we also have the *Irish Catholic Catechism for Adults* (2014). The processes, structures and content have been made clear. This welcome new book is a helpful manual that examines how the mission of evangelisation takes place in the concrete realities of daily encounters. The author has long experience of celebrating and sharing the Gospel and I welcome his timely contribution to the exciting mission of helping others to encounter *Christ himself, who is to be known, loved and imitated.*

Donal McKeown, bishop of Derry
(Chairman of the Irish Episcopal Commission for Worship, Pastoral Renewal and Faith Development).

Introduction

In mid June 2008 four members of the Alpha board in Ireland were prompted, hopefully by the Holy Spirit, to invite interested people to join them on four successive Sunday nights to pray for revival and renewal in the Church.

When the four weeks had passed, the meetings continued by common agreement. Sometime later the eighteen or so participants acknowledged that they were becoming a community with a common sense of purpose. As a result they wrote a mission statement which expressed their core vision in these words, 'With the help of the Holy Spirit, we will engage in evangelisation ourselves, as well as teaching, training and equipping others who also desire to evangelise those who have not yet developed an intimate personal relationship with Jesus as their Lord and Saviour.'

In May 2009 the members of the nascent community were led by the Spirit to call themselves the New Springtime Community and to choose the buttercup as their logo. Sometime later a team of four was elected to lead the community for a renewable period of three years. In 2011 the members agreed that they would commit their energies primarily, though not exclusively, to one or other of three interconnected streams; 1) Evangelising; 2) Formation for evangelisation; 3) Intercessory Prayer.

TRAINING FOR EVANGELISATION

The church and Recent Popes have spoken about the need to train those who want to engage in the new evangelisation.
- Pope Paul VI said in par. 73 of *Evangelisation in the Modern World*, 'A serious preparation is needed for all workers for evangelisation.'
- Pope John Paul II said in par. 46 of *The Church in Europe*, 'evangelisers must be properly trained... All the baptised, since they are witnesses of Christ, should receive a training appropriate to their circumstances.'
- Pope Francis said in par. 121 of *The Joy of the Gospel*, 'All of us are called to mature in our work as evangelisers. We want to have better training, a deepening love and a clearer witness to the Gospel.' However, he added in par. 120, 'Anyone who has truly experienced God's saving love does not need much time or lengthy training to go out and proclaim that love.'
- Proposition 46 of the 2012 post synodal document, *The New Evangelisation for the Transmission of the Christian Faith* says, 'This Synod considers that it is necessary to establish formation centres for the New Evangelisation, where lay people learn how to speak of the person of Christ in a persuasive manner adapted to our time and to specific groups of people, e.g., young adults, agnostics, the elderly and so forth.' Proposition 9 of the document said that the church should produce resources which could be used to

train evangelisers, 'The Synod Fathers propose that guidelines of the initial proclamation of the kerygma be written. This compendium would include:
- Systematic teaching on the kerygma in the Scriptures and Tradition of the Catholic Church
- Teachings and quotations from the missionary saints and martyrs in our Catholic history that would assist us in our pastoral challenges of today
- Qualities and guidelines for the formation of Catholic evangelisers today.'

Speaking about formation for evangelisation the mission statement of the New Springtime Community states, 'we will put on practical courses that will teach lay people about the nature, motives and means of engaging in the new evangelisation.' To this end we designed a six session long *Parish Evangelisation Course*, and a certificate course which includes 26 sessions. It has been taught on a number of occasions in Dublin, and in a modified form in Prague, in the Czech Republic, and Palermo, in Sicily. This book is based on the longer version of that course and is in conformity with another line in our mission statement which states that the community will 'publish written and electronic resource materials.'

Purpose of the book
In recent years the Irish Episcopal Conference published, *Share the Good News: National Directory for Catechesis in Ireland* (Dublin: Veritas, 2010). The bishops also asked the Council for Pastoral Renewal and Faith Development to set up a task group to make

recommendations on evangelisation. I was a member of that group. It's work finally bore fruit when the Irish Episcopal conference published, *Evangelise Today, Sharing The Good News of Jesus Christ: Reflections and Resources for Practitioners* (Dublin: Veritas, 2014). It is my hope that this book will augment those primary resources in a practical way.

Readers will notice that there are many quotations peppered throughout the book which are taken from Church teaching and the writings of recent popes. The reason for doing this is threefold. Firstly, whereas a lot of writing on religious topics is based on human speculation, that of the Church is authoritative and reliable. As par 10 of the Dogmatic Constitution on *Divine Revelation* said, 'The task of authoritatively interpreting the word of God, whether written or handed on [Scripture or Tradition], has been entrusted exclusively to the living *magisterium* of the Church, whose authority is exercised in the name of Jesus Christ.' Secondly, anyone who reads what the Church has to say about evangelisation will find that it is at once insightful, from a theological point of view, and practical, from a pastoral perspective. For example, speaking about Paul VI's *Evangelisation in the Modern World*, Pope Francis has said, 'to my mind it is the greatest pastoral document that has ever been written to this day.' In the minds of many, his own apostolic declaration, *The Joy of the Gospel*, is a contender for the number two spot. Thirdly, it is a pity that so many Catholics, both clerical and lay, do not have a detailed and nuanced knowledge of the profound teaching of the Church on the new evangelisation. This book aims to help its readers to become more familiar with it.

INTRODUCTION

It is worth mentioning in passing, that because of the constrictions of space, a number of interesting and relevant topics had to be overlooked such as, popular piety and evangelisation, evangelisation and the social media, evangelising and ministry in the streets etc. I have briefly discussed some of those subjects in *The Gifts of the Spirit and the New Evangelisation* (Dublin: Columba, 2009) and *Basic Evangelisation: Guidelines for Catholics* (Dublin: Columba, 2010).

This book is aimed at a wide range of possible readers such as those who have attended theological, and adult faith education courses of one kind or another and who desire to put their knowledge to good use. Hopefully, it will also be helpful for clergy, religious, people belonging to parish pastoral councils, members of prayer and evangelising groups, the Vincent de Paul Society, the Legion of Mary, as well as other interested church groups and individuals such as those who have attended a Life in the Spirit Seminar, or an Alpha Course. Each of our certificate course meetings includes four components:

- Opening prayer
- Content
- Suggested questions for reflection and/or discussion
- Prayer Response

However, for the sake of brevity, this book will only include the content and reflection questions. It is hoped that besides informing its readers *Encountering Jesus* will be a practical resource for anyone who wants to run a training course on the new evangelisation in a diocese or a parish. The same fourfold structure, already mentioned, could be used and modified in creative ways to suit the needs of those attending. For example, the opening prayer could be replaced by some hymns. The content could be presented as a power point presentation. The questions suggested here for reflection and discussion are indicative rather than prescriptive. They could be augmented or replaced by others. The prayer response, could take a number of forms, including praying for one another. The layout of the book is intended to make it easy to understand and to use as a teaching resource.

Conclusion

I want to express my heartfelt thanks to the members of the New Springtime Community for all the selfless contributions they have made to the running and development of the certificate course. Sr. Jane Ford of the Holy Faith sisters, deserves a special word of appreciation for all the work she has done as a speaker, administrator and general *factotum*.On behalf of the community, I not only want to thank our guest speakers, who so generously shared their knowledge and expertise with us, but also the many men and women who attended the course and enriched it by their questions, insights and enthusiasm. Last, but not least I want to thank the most reverend Dr. Dónal McKeown, bishop of Derry, and Chairman of the Council for Pastoral Renewal and Adult Faith Development in Ireland for agreeing to write the foreword.

As early as 1990 St. John Paul II said in par. 3 of *The Mission of the Redeemer,* 'I sense that the moment has come to commit all of the Church's energies to a new evangelisation.' A lot of water has flowed under the bridge since those words were spoken. No wonder Pope Francis asked in par. 120 of *The Joy of the Gospel,* 'What are we waiting for?'

Section One:

Prologue

ONE

THE NEED FOR EVANGELISATION

In 1969 Fr. Joseph Ratzinger, who would later become Pope Benedict XVI, spoke about the possible future of the Church on German radio. He began his talk by saying, 'The theologian is no soothsayer, nor is he a futurologist who makes a calculation of the future based on the measureable facts of the present.' His prescient text has since been published in a book entitled, *Faith and the Future* (San Francisco: Ignatius Press, 2009). Among other things he said that in the future the Church would go through a painful time of purification. 'It will become small and will have to start pretty much all over again. It will no longer have use of the structures it built in its years of prosperity. The reduction in the number of faithful will lead to it losing an important part of its social privileges.' Renewal will start off with small groups and movements and a minority that will make faith central to experience again. 'It will be a more spiritual Church, and will not claim a political mandate flirting with the Right one minute and the Left the next. It will be poor and will become the Church of the destitute.' He added, 'As a small society, [the Church] will make much bigger demands on the initiative of her individual members.'

Ratzinger said that the process he had outlined would be a 'long' one 'but when all the suffering is past, a great power will emerge from a more spiritual and simple Church, at which point humans will realise that they live in a world of indescribable solitude and having lost sight of God they will perceive the horror of their poverty.' Then and only then, Ratzinger concluded, will they see 'the small flock of the faithful as something completely new: they will see it as a source of hope for themselves, the answer they had always secretly been searching for.'

On the Monday following Pentecost in 1975, Ratzinger's words seemed to be confirmed by two interrelated prophecies which were spoken in St. Peter's Basilica in Rome, by Americans Ralph Martin and Bruce Yocum. Pope Paul VI was present. They seemed to contain a number of distinct but interrelated points.

ROMAN PROPHECY: PHASE ONE
Firstly, the Lord seemed to predict that a time of purifying darkness was about to afflict the church. 'Open your eyes, open your hearts to prepare yourselves for me and for the day that I have now begun. My church will be different; my people will be different; difficulties and trials will come upon you. I will lead you into the desert, I will strip you of everything that you are depending on now, so you depend just on me.' The Lord went on to say more about the purpose of the time of trial and purification. 'You need the power of my Holy Spirit in a way that you have not possessed it; you need an understanding of my will and of the ways I work that you do not yet have'

Would it not be true to say that the prediction about darkness in the Church is being fulfilled. It has been afflicted ever since the prophecies were spoken. It is, as if the powers of hell have been released in order to mount an attack on the people of God. In a homily given by Paul VI on the 29th of June, 1972, he said that he had a feeling that, 'from some fissure the smoke of Satan has entered into the temple of God.' One is reminded in this context of words spoken by Jesus, 'behold, Satan demanded to have you, that he might sift you like wheat' (Lk 22:31). The effects have been obvious. Many people have drifted away in the day of testing. In places such as Europe, the U.S.A., and Australia practice rates, together with vocations to the priesthood and religious life, have fallen rapidly for many reasons.

When Pope John Paul II came to the Republic of Ireland in 1979, about 87% of Catholics attended weekly Mass. In an interview published in the March 2015 issue of *U.S. Catholic* magazine (Vol. 80, No. 3), Archbishop Diarmuid Martin of Dublin said, 'Only about 20 or 25 percent of the Irish population go to Mass every Sunday and have some real sense of commitment to the church.' At the end of 2011 it was estimated that the overall practice rate in the Archdiocese of Dublin was as low as 14%. In some parishes it has fallen to 2 or 3%. The Gallup International Association poll of 2011, titled the *Global Index of Religion and Atheism*, asked 50,000 people in 57 countries: 'Irrespective of whether you attend a place of worship or not, would you say you are a religious person, not a religious person or a convinced atheist?' In 2011, 47% of Irish respondents said they considered themselves religious, 44% not religious, and 10% convinced atheists. When asked in a 2015 referendum whether they wanted gay marriage, over 60% of the largely Catholic population voted yes in spite of the fact that the Church was against it. It would seem that the 'silent apostasy' referred to by Pope John Paul II in par. 9 of *The Church in Europe*, is taking place not only in continental Europe but in Ireland as well.

One of the reasons for the lack of religious conviction is the fact that there is a faith crisis of head, heart and hands.

a. The faith crisis of the head

This crisis of the head has to do with knowledge. Many Catholics are unaware of the core teachings of the Christian faith. Some of them espouse ideas which are contrary to church teaching such as occult, superstitious and New Age beliefs and practices like Reiki, Tarot, angelology, having recourse to crystals, mediums, spiritualists etc. St. John Paul II went even further when he stated in par. 9 of The Church in Europe, 'European culture gives the impression of silent apostasy on the part of people who have all that they need and who live as if God does not exist.'

b. The Faith crisis of the heart

The crisis of the heart has to do with experience. Even if some Catholics know a good deal about the person of Jesus many of them don't know him in person. This could be due to

- lack of personal faith,
- A negative image of God,

- An unwillingness to turn away from sin,
- Or some other personal reason.

This lack of conscious awareness of the person of Jesus and of the free, unmerited gift of his forgiveness and love is often evident in a lack of inner peace and joy.

c. The faith crisis of the hands

The faith crisis of the hands has to do with Christian action. If the truth of the gospel has not fallen from the head to the heart, it is not surprising that Catholics often fail to act in a way that would be consistent with the teachings of Christ and his church. For example, in recent years this has been particularly obvious in the realms of sexual and business morality where many people have re-written the commandments to suit themselves. In this connection one is reminded of the words of Judges 21:25, 'In those days there was no king in Israel. Everyone did what was right in his own eyes.' Although current statistics indicate that Ireland is still a Christian country it won't be for long if current trends continue. What is clearly needed is what is referred to as a new evangelisation.

ROMAN PROPHECY: PHASE TWO

The prophecy given in St Peter's in 1975 seemed to say that the time of darkness in the church would be followed by a time of darkness in the secular world. It predicted that, 'Days of darkness are coming on the world, days of tribulation.' I have believed for many years now, that a time is coming when there will be great disruption and even breakdown in the secular world.

In a book entitled, *Unveiling the Heart* (Dublin: Veritas, 1995), I predicted on page forty nine that the breakdown could take the form of an economic collapse. Incidentally, I found out sometime later that in 1985 Cardinal Ratzinger had made a similar prediction in a paper entitled, *Market Economy and Ethics*. He warned that a lack of ethics, 'can actually cause the laws of the market to collapse.' When Leehman Brothers imploded in 2008, I thought, 'there we go, the economic dominoes are beginning to fall.' I believe that, there is still another very difficult time of disruption yet to come. For example, on Sept. 14th 2014, Pope Francis said in a homily that Word War III has already begun, 'Even today, after the failure of a second world war, perhaps one can speak of a third war, one fought piecemeal, with crimes, massacres, and destruction.' Whenever and however affliction occurs, it will cause some people to say, 'let us eat, drink and be merry for tomorrow we die!' (cf. Eccl 8:15) and others to say, 'let us seek the Lord while he may still be found?' (Is 55:6). At the moment there are wars and rumours of wars (Mt 24:6) and many other dangers. Where will they lead?

ROMAN PROPHECY: PHASE THREE

This brings us to a third point in the prophecy. The Lord intends to use the army of committed followers who he has been raising up and equipping during the Church's time of darkness to evangelise those who will seek him during the time of darkness in the secular world. As the Lord said in the prophecy in St. Peter's, 'I will prepare you for a time of evangelism that the world has not seen.' It is my belief that in God's good time it will bring about the new springtime for Christianity which was referred to by Pope John Paul II and his successor, Benedict XVI.

Need for new evangelisation

What the Church has perceived so clearly is that a new evangelisation is needed. Pope John Paul II said in par. 34 of his apostolic exhortation, *The Vocation And The Mission of the Lay Faithful*, 'Whole countries and nations where religion and the Christian life were formerly flourishing and capable of fostering a viable and working community of faith, are now put to a hard test, and in some cases, are even undergoing a radical transformation, as a result of a constant spreading of an indifference to religion, of secularism and atheism. This particularly concerns countries and nations of the so-called First World, in which economic well-being and consumerism, even if coexistent with a tragic situation of poverty and misery, inspires and sustains a life lived 'as if God did not exist.' The new evangelisation is responding to this challenge and seeking to restore and renew the faith of those who may be 'baptised pagans.' Happily this is happening nowadays for an ever increasing number of people. It is often the result of being evangelised by a committed Christian or attending such things as an Alpha Course, a Life in the Spirit Seminar, or a Cursillo Weekend. As a result, many Catholics are experiencing a spiritual awakening. We are being prepared to be counted among those who will bring about the New Springtime.

Suggested questions for reflection and/or discussion

1. Do you think that is true to say that, currently, there is a faith crisis of head, heart and hands?

2. What is your reaction to the prophecies referred to in this chapter?

3. Do you feel an inner call to share the Good News about Jesus with other people?

TWO

MODELS OF EVANGELISATION

In the 1980's I preached a lot of retreats to priests, nuns and lay people. At the time I noticed that, while some people really liked what I had to say, there were others who were not nearly as enthusiastic. For a period, I wondered why this was so. Then I came across a chapter in a book which described three models of spirituality. It made complete sense of what I had been experiencing. It was clear that the content of my preaching had been informed by a pneumatic/charismatic model of spirituality. As a result, the listeners who espoused the same model liked what I had to say, while those who espoused different models, were not nearly as appreciative. Later I found that Cardinal Avery Dulles had been the first Catholic theologian who had used models, or ideal types, to clarify people's different approaches to religious topics. He did so notably in his influential book *Models of the Church* (Dublin: Gill & Macmillan, 1988). In this chapter we are going to apply his approach to evangelisation.

MODELS: THEIR NATURE AND PURPOSE

The notion of models is borrowed from the world of science.
- Models are ideal cases which make it possible to notice and interpret certain important aspects of experience.

- The models are descriptive rather than evaluative.
- All of them are valid up to a certain extent, and have their own distinctive strengths and weaknesses.
- While everyone is mainly committed to one particular model, he or she usually augments it with elements from the other models.

In this chapter I am going to suggest that there are three models of evangelisation.

1. THE DIDACTIC/SACRAMENTAL MODEL

Didactic/sacramental evangelisation focuses on the head and is mainly concerned with *orthodoxy*, i.e., right teaching. Adherents of this model, presuppose that Catholics are already evangelised as a result of receiving the sacraments of baptism and confirmation and living in the Christian community.

When I was conducting parish missions in the 1980s and 90s I could see that we missioners were presuming that the people were evangelised. As a result we saw evangelisation mainly as catechesis, i.e., instructing people in the doctrinal and moral teachings of the Church. We would give sermons on topics such as prayer, coping with suffering, the Eucharist, family life, devotion to our Lady etc. This kind of instruction was didactic and often lacked an experiential or personal dimension.

Evangelisation in this model was also seen as sacramental ministry, as a means of grace and growth. While it is true that sacraments are objective means of grace (*ex opere operato* in

Latin), we can only receive that grace in so far as we are subjectively open to it by means of personal faith (*Ex opere operantis* in Latin).

This model has obvious strengths.
- It is traditional and has worked well in the past.
- The fact that it stresses the importance of objective truth gives it a sense of clarity and reliability in our relativistic culture.
- This approach does not presuppose that people have a developed sense of self-awareness, or much education.
- It stresses that perfection is largely a matter of obedience, i.e., believing and doing what the Church teaches from a doctrinal and moral point of view.

The didactic/sacramental model of evangelisation also has clear weaknesses.
- It wrongly pre-supposes that people are fully evangelised and have a faith-filled relationship with the person of Jesus Christ. Consequently, the catechesis and sacramental ministry they receive often bear surprisingly little fruit because they are built on sand.
- Sociological research confirms the fact that, because of its objective, ritualistic approach, the didactic/sacramental model is often not very effective in the subjective, experiential type of culture in which we live.

2. THE KERYGMATIC/CHARISMATIC MODEL
The Kerygmatic/charismatic model of evangelisation focuses

on the heart, and is mainly concerned with *orthokardia*, i.e., right experience. This model of evangelisation is informed by the belief that faith is primarily a matter of trust in God. Consequently, there is a strong appreciation of the need for primary or kerygmatic evangelisation where the aim is to lead people to the experience of Christ centered salvation. It aims to bring people into a heartfelt awareness of God, and God's forgiveness and love (Eph 3:14-18). The Irish bishops described this grace in a pastoral letter entitled *Life in the Spirit* (Dublin: Veritas, 1993) as, 'a conversion gift through which one receives a new and significant commitment to the Lordship of Jesus, and an openness to the power and gifts of the Holy Spirit.' In this regard, Fr Raniero Cantalamessa, the papal preacher, cites the example of John Wesley, the founder of Methodism. Having experienced a personal faith crisis, he heard someone talking about the topic of justification at a prayer meeting in London. It had a profound effect. He wrote, 'I felt that I did trust in Christ, Christ alone for my salvation, And an inner assurance was given to me that he had taken away all my sins, even mine and saved me from the law of sin and death.' Clearly, the truth about God's saving love had fallen the vital eighteen inches from his head to his heart.

Pentecostals and Charismatics believe that the preaching of the core Christian teachings must be backed up with personal testimony, i.e., how the preacher or teacher has experienced it's saving truth him or herself. Pentecostals and Charismatics also believe that the message of salvation can be demonstrated occasionally by means of the charisms of power such as healing.

Afterwards this conversion experience is expressed in a changed way of living as a disciple of the Lord.

The kerygmatic-charismatic approach has a number of strengths.
- It stresses the primary importance of faith in the person of Jesus Christ and his willingness to forgive all our sins. This model of evangelisation is intensely personal, and experiential. As such, it is suited to the needs and expectations of the experiential culture in which we live.
- Whereas didactic-sacramental evangelisation has often produced disappointing results in the contemporary Church, this approach has been more successful in renewing faith and commitment as Church statistician David Barrett's ecclesiastical figures have shown. By and large the communities that are gaining new members are those which adopt this approach.

It goes without saying that the kerygmatic-charismatic approach to evangelisation has certain weaknesses.
- It can tend towards individualism by stressing, 'my salvation,' 'my experience,' thereby neglecting the community dimension of the Christian life.
- It can underestimate the importance of the sacraments while tending toward subjectivism, whereby people place more confidence in their own feelings and experiences such as dreams, visions, inspirations and prophecies than in the official teaching of the Church, which can be overlooked rather than rejected.

- It can adopt a narrow view of evangelisation, one which may overlook the importance of the socio-cultural aspects of the Christian life, such as action for justice, transformation of the culture, protecting the environment etc.

3. THE POLITICAL/DEVELOPMENTAL MODEL

Political/Developmental evangelisation focuses on the hands and is mainly concerned with *orthopraxis*, i.e., right action. This model is informed by the belief that faith is primarily a matter of remedial action on behalf of the less well off and oppressed. As scripture reminds us, 'faith by itself, if it is not accompanied by action, is dead' (Jm 2:17). It sees Jesus as an exemplar of this approach to evangelisation, a liberator who came to set people free from all that oppressed them, whether personal sin or the unjust structures of society, e.g., when Jesus cleansed the temple by chasing out the unjust moneychangers and those selling sacrifical animals for extortionate sums of money.

This model of evangelisation is pragmatic in orientation, relatively new, and owes a good deal to the liberation theology which has been developed in third world countries, especially in South America, afflicted, as it is, by socio-economic injustice. It has also been influenced by new insights in Catholic social teaching, e.g., Pope Paul VI's encyclical, *The Development of Peoples* (1967); as well as Marxist thinking and the human sciences.

In this model it is assumed that Christ is already with the poor, and that evangelisation is helping them to recognise and affirm their already existing dignity as children of God. It also helps to liberate them from any evils which would be alien to their Christian dignity. These needs are identified by means of social analysis, and they are challenged and changed both by means of merciful deeds and action for justice. By showing compassion and love in these practical ways, not only do these evangelists witness to the Good News, they themselves are evangelised in the process. Their solidarity with the poor is the indispensable interpretative key that enables them to unlock the spiritual riches of the scriptures which are Good News for the poor.

This praxis approach to evangelisation has a number of strengths.
- It seems to have influenced the apostolic exhortation of Pope Francis, *The Joy of the Gospel*, e.g., pars 186-216 and his encyclical *On Care for our Common Home*.
- It is relevant to the needs of our time especially in poorer countries. It is practical in orientation and is motivated by important biblical themes, e.g., 'blessed are the poor' (Lk 6:20), and 'as often as you do it to the least, you do it to me,' (Mt 25:40) etc.
- Besides alleviating the evils associated with poverty, it also tackles its systemic causes.

The political/developmental approach to evangelisation also has a number of weaknesses.
- It can neglect the importance of personal commitment to Christ
- It can be Pelagian by being self-reliant and too human-

istic, substituting political liberty for religious self-transcendence.
- As Cardinal Dulles has remarked, this model of evangelisation is novel and has not been well tested.

EVALUATION

Which of these models of evangelisation is best suited to meet the needs of our culture? Because the didactic/sacramental model of evangelisation is objective and abstract in a subjective experiential culture, it is not well adapted to the needs of the time. However the kerygmatic/charismatic and the political/developmental models of evangelisation are both pragmatic and experiential in orientation and therefore more attuned to the modern mind set. Which of them is to be favoured? It is arguable that in the New Testament there is a logical theological sequence in the types of evangelisation. The kerygmatic/charismatic model with its emphasis on conversion to Christ and deeds of power, would be the logical one to start with. Then it could be augmented with relevant aspects, firstly of the didactic/sacramental and then the praxis/developmental models. That said, no matter what model a person consciously or unconsciously espouses can be augmented with good elements from the other two.

Suggested questions for reflection and/or discussion

1. Did you find that the description of the three models of evangelisation was helpful?

2. Having read about the three models of evangelisation, to which one do you think that you mainly belong? Why?

3. What aspects of the other two models would you wish to adopt?

Section Two:

Evangelisation and New Evangelisation

THREE

EVANGELISATION: IT'S NATURE AND MOTIVES

Although many contemporary Catholics associate evangelisation with Protestantism, in fact the word and activity have their origins in the New Testament. There the Greek word *euangelion*, means 'good news' So evangelisation means 'to announce the good news.'

While the subject of evangelisation was hardly mentioned at Vatican I (1869-70), it was referred to many times at Vatican II (1962-65). It marked the end of the counter Reformation and inaugerated a paradigm shift in the Catholic Church, one that would put more emphasis on the word of God, the Holy Spirit and evangelisation. Since the end of the Council, the Popes have drawn out the implications of its teachings for mission. In par. 14 of *Evangelisation in the Modern World* Bl. Paul VI said, 'The task of evangelising all people constitutes the essential mission of the Church... She exists in order to evangelise.'

In par. 18 of *Evangelisation in the Modern World* Paul VI offered his only definition of the activity when he wrote, 'The Church evangelises when she seeks to convert, solely through the divine power of the message she proclaims, both the personal and collective consciences of people, the activities in which they engage, and the lives and concrete milieu which are theirs.' Pope Francis added in par. 14 of *The Joy of the Gospel*, 'Evangelisation is first and foremost about preaching the Gospel to those who do not know Jesus Christ or who have always rejected him.' I once heard it said that evangelisation is one beggar telling another where he or she has found the bread of life.

Current church documents make it clear that evangelisation is not synonymous with *foreign* missions. There is also a pressing need for *home* missions. The traditional, long-accepted division of the world into Christian countries and mission lands, despite its conceptual clarity, is now seen as limited, overly simple and no longer applicable to the present situation.

FORMS OF EVANGELISATION

Church documents point out that evangelisation can take many forms such as pre-evangelisation, initial evangelisation, catechesis, apologetics, inculturation, inter-religious dialogue, action for justice and ecumenism. Let's look at what official church documents say about them in a little more detail.

1. Pre-evangelisation

It involves living in the midst of the people to be evangelised and witnessing to the Gospel, wordlessly, by the way one lives. For a vivid example of this, see the French movie *Of Gods and Men*. It is about French Trappists who lived, served and died as martyrs among the Moslems of Algeria. They had witnessed to the Word without speaking a word to them (cf. 1 Pt 3:1).

2. Kerygmatic or primary evangelisation

The *kerygma* is the proclamation of the central and core Gospel message of salvation. Speaking about it, in par. 44 of the *Mission of the Redeemer,* John Paul II wrote, 'initial proclamation has a central and irreplaceable role, since it introduces man 'into the mystery of the love of God, who invites him to enter into a personal relationship with himself in Christ.' In par. 164 of *The Joy of the Gospel* Pope Francis wrote, 'This first proclamation is called 'first' not because it exists at the beginning and can then be forgotten or replaced by other more important things. It is first in a qualitative sense because it is the principal proclamation, the one which we must hear again and again in different ways, the one which we must announce one way or another throughout the process of catechesis, at every level and moment.'

3. Catechesis

This form of Christian instruction builds on the kerygma by teaching people what disciples believe and how they live. Par. 61 of the *General Directory for Catechesis* says that, catechesis, 'distinct from the primary proclamation of the Gospel, promotes and matures initial conversion, educates the convert to the faith and incorporates him or her into the Christian community.'

4. Apologetics

The English word is derived from Greek and means, 'speaking in defence.' Apologetics defends the reasonableness of faith. Speaking in Washington in 2010, Pope Benedict XVI said, 'In a society that rightly values personal liberty, the church needs to promote at every level of her teaching – in catechesis, preaching, seminary and university instruction – an apologetics aimed at affirming the truth of Christian revelation, the harmony of faith and reason, and a sound understanding of freedom, seen in positive terms as a liberation both from the limitations of sin and for an authentic and fulfilling life.' Pope Francis talked about the relationship of science and faith in pars 242-243 of *The Joy of the Gospel*.

5. Inculturation

Evangelisation seeks to relate Christian truth to contemporary culture while seeking to change the culture in the light of those truths. In par. 52 of the *Mission of the Redeemer* John Paul said that inculturation, 'means the intimate transformation of authentic cultural values through their integration in Christianity and the insertion of Christianity in the various human cultures.' In secularised societies there is always a temptation to try to adapt the gospel to contemporary culture. Pope John Paul II used to speak of *areopagi*, places where believers could dialogue with those who were seeking meaning with sincere hearts (cf. Acts 17:24). Pope Benedict used a similar image when he talked about the *court of the gentiles* where believers could discuss issues with unbelievers (cf. Acts 21: 27-32).

6. Inter-religious dialogue

It is talking to people of other faiths in order to discover common ground and to demonstrate how Christian truth fulfils all that is best in those faiths. In par. 55 of *The Church in Europe* John Paul wrote, 'As is the case with the overall commitment to the 'new evangelisation, so too proclaiming the Gospel of hope calls for the establishment of a profound and perceptive inter-religious dialogue, particularly with Judaism and with Islam.' Pope Francis talked about this subject in pars 250-254 of *The Joy of the Gospel*.

7. Action for justice
In 1971 a document entitled, *Justice in the World*, which was published by a synod of bishops, we read, 'Action on behalf of justice and participation in the transformation of the world fully appear as a constitutive dimension of the preaching of the gospel.' Writing in par. 15 of his encyclical *Charity in Truth*, Pope Benedict wrote, 'Paul VI clearly presented the relationship between the proclamation of Christ and the advancement of the individual in society. Testimony to Christ's charity, through works of justice, peace and development, is part and parcel of evangelisation.' Pope Francis talked on the same subject in chapter four of *The Joy of the Gospel* pars 177-258.

8. Ecumenism
Echoing what other Pontiffs have said, Pope Francis wrote in par 244 of *The Joy of the Gospel*, 'The credibility of the Christian message would be much greater if Christians could overcome their divisions and the Church could realise 'the fullness of catholicity proper to her in those of her children who, though joined to her by baptism, are yet separated from full communion with her.' This subject is dealt with at greater length in chapter sixteen.

It is important, not to understand evangelisation as being solely identified with any one or other of these eight activities.

Motives for Evangelising

The primary motive for evangelisation is the great comission of Jesus when he sent the apostles and disciples out to evangelise, e.g., in Mt 28:18-20. Pope Francis said in par. 49 of *The Joy of the Gospel*, 'If something should rightly disturb us and trouble our consciences, it is the fact that so many of our brothers and sisters are living without the strength, light and consolation born of friendship with Jesus Christ, without a community of faith to support them, without meaning and a goal in life.' Founder of the Legion of Mary, venerable Frank Duff, said in 1948, 'An inert laity is only two generations removed from non-practice, non-practice is only two generations away from non-belief.'

In pars 61-64 of *Mission of the Reedemer* Pope John Paul II proposed six motives for evangelisation. Surprisingly, he didn't seem to stress the need for evangelisation in order to help people to escape the pains of eternal separation from God. However, it is worth remembering that Jesus said, 'Enter through the narrow gate. For wide is the gate and broad is the road that leads to destruction, and many enter through it. But small is the gate and narrow the road that leads to life, and only a few find it' (Mt 7:13-14). Given that this is the case, many people may be in trouble, so evangelisers, like Jesus the good shepherd, seek out those who are in danger of being lost.

Conclusion

We conclude by quoting some striking words from a talk of Pope Francis, 'I want to tell you something. In the Gospel there's that beautiful passage that tells us of the shepherd who, on returning to the sheepfold and realising that a sheep is missing, leaves the 99 and goes to look for it, to look for the one. But, brothers and sisters, we have one. It's the 99 who we're missing! We have to go out, we must go to them! In this culture - let's face it - we only have one. We are the minority. And do we feel the fervour, the apostolic zeal to go out and find the other 99? This is a big responsibility and we must ask the Lord for the grace of generosity and the courage and the patience to go out, to go out and proclaim the Gospel.'

Suggested questions for reflection and/or discussion

- Is your parish inward or outward looking, devoted mainly to maintenance or mission?

- Eight forms of evangelisation were mentioned. Which one attracts you the most?

- Why should lay Catholics want to evangelise?

FOUR

THE NEW EVANGELISATION EXPLAINED

In his book *Crossing the Threshold of Hope* (London: Jonathan Cape, 1994), John Paul II said that the gathering of the bishops in Rome between 1962-5, 'had a fundamental importance for evangelisation, for the new evangelisation originated precisely at the Second Vatican Council.' He first used the words new evangelisation in the course of a homily delivered in Poland in 1979, 'the Gospel is again being proclaimed. *A new evangelisation* has begun, as if it were a new proclamation, even if in reality it is the same as ever.'

NEW IN ARDOUR, METHODS AND FORMS OF EXPRESSION

In 1983 John Paul said to the bishops in Latin America, 'The commemoration of this half millennium of evangelisation will have full significance if, as bishops, with your priests and faithful, you accept it as your commitment; a commitment not of re-evangelisation, but rather of a new evangelisation; new in its ardour, methods and forms of expression.'

- Speaking about the new ardour that is needed, John Paul II said par. 40 of *At the Beginning of the New Millennium*, 'We must rekindle in ourselves the impetus of

the beginnings and allow ourselves to be filled with the ardour of the apostolic preaching which followed Pentecost. We must revive in ourselves the burning conviction of Paul, who cried out: 'Woe to me if I do not preach the Gospel'
- There are many *new methods* that can be used to evangelise such as street evangelism, evangelisation courses such as Life in the Spirit seminars and Alpha, and using creative ideas to attract lapsed Catholics such as having a Christmas party to which everyone in the area is invited.
- There are also many *new ways of expressing* the Christian message such as the internet, social media, mime, Radio, drama, music, DVDs and the like.

New Evangelisation defined

While the gospel message is not new, the culture in which it is proclaimed is changing all the time. As a result, Christians have to find innovative ways of communicating the Gospel at a time when so many people live as if God does not exist. In the *Instrumentum Laboris* in preparation for the 2012 Synod on the new evangelisation, the concept was defined in proposition 85 as follows, 'The phrase 'new evangelisation' designates pastoral outreach to those who no longer practice the Christian faith.' When the 2012 synod of bishops ended, Cardinal Donald Wuerl, its relator general, defined the New Evangelisation as follows, 'At its heart the New Evangelisation is the re-proposing of the encounter with the Risen Lord, his Gospel, and his Church to those who no longer find the Church's message engaging.'

The New Evangelisation is Radically Christ Centred

Papal preacher, Raniero Cantalamessa has observed in the opening chapter of *Remember Jesus Christ* (Frederick: Word Among Us Press, 2007), that many Catholics are deists but not fully Christian. They believe in God's existence while having little or no relationship with Jesus Christ. However, since the end of the Vatican Council we have become increasingly Christ centred. That is clear in Church teaching. Here are some examples.

- In par. 22 of *Evangelisation in the Modern World* Paul VI said, 'There is no true evangelisation if the name, the teaching, the life, the promises, the kingdom and the mystery of Jesus of Nazareth, the Son of God are not proclaimed.'
- Pope John Paul focused attention on the Christocentric nature of evangelisation when he said in 1992 to the bishops of Southern Germany, 'It is necessary to awaken in believers a full relationship with Christ, mankind's only Saviour. Only from a personal relationship with Jesus can an effective evangelisation develop.'
- Pope Benedict XVI said on Sept. 3rd, 2008, 'Christianity is not a new philosophy or new morality. We are Christians only if we encounter Christ... Only in this personal relationship with Christ, only in this encounter with the Risen One do we really become Christians... Therefore, let us pray to the Lord to enlighten us, so that, in our world, he will grant us the encounter with his

presence, and thus give us a lively faith, an open heart, and great charity for all, capable of renewing the world.'
- Pope Francis said in par. 110 of *The Joy of the Gospel*, 'there can be no true evangelisation without the explicit proclamation of Jesus as Lord,' and without 'the primacy of the proclamation of Jesus Christ in all evangelising work.'

It would probably be true to say that the new evangelisation is mainly, though by no means exclusively, focused on evangelisation of a kerygmatic kind.

WHO ARE THE FOCUS OF THE NEW EVANGELISATION?

The Church believes that the parish as a community of communities is the focal point of the new evangelisation. It concentrates its main efforts on two distinct groups of people.

Firstly, there are the many men and women who have been baptised and perhaps confirmed but who do not attend church, know very little about Christian teaching, and are often influenced by occult and new age beliefs and non-Christian moral mores. They are referred to as the un-churched or the lapsed. Pope Benedict has said that the new evangelisation is directed,' principally at those who, though baptised, have drifted away from the Church and live without reference to the Christian life.' The new evangelisation aims to, 'help these people encounter the Lord, who alone fills our existence with deep meaning and peace.'

Secondly, there are people who are sometimes referred to as cultural Catholics. Although they go to church on a regular basis, and are sacramentalised and catechised, nevertheless many of them are not yet fully evangelised. They are like the dutiful elder bother in the parable of the Prodigal Son. Although they go to church they do not seem to realise that the Father is saying to them, 'all I have is yours' (Lk 15:31) e.g., the power and gifts of the Holy Spirit. To use a phrase of John Paul II, in par. 19 of *On Catechesis in our Time*, they have not yet crossed 'the threshold of faith' to form 'an explicit personal attachment to Jesus Christ.' The new evangelisation seeks to help them to cross that threshold.

WHO ENGAGES IN THE NEW EVANGELISATION?

Only those who have been truly evangelised themselves will have the desire and ability to evangelise others. In par. 24 of *Evangelisation in the Modern World*, Pope Paul VI said in a striking way, 'the person who has been evangelised goes on to evangelise others. Here lies the test of truth, the touchstone of evangelisation: it is unthinkable that a person should accept the Word and give himself to the kingdom without becoming a person who bears witness to it and proclaims it in his turn.'

a. Clergy

In par 3 of the *Decree on the Ministry and Life of Priests*, we read, 'Since no one can be saved who does not first believe, priests, as co-workers with their bishops, have the primary duty of proclaiming the Gospel of God to all.' In chapter one, section two of a document entitled, *The Priest and the Third Millenium*, which was published by the Congregation for the Clergy in 1999, we are told about the role of clergy in the new evangelisation, 'While the pastors of the Church know that they themselves were not established by Christ to undertake alone the whole of the salvific mission of the Church to the world, they do exercise an absolutely indispensable evangelising role. New evangelisation needs urgently to find a form for the exercise of the priestly ministry really consonant with contemporary conditions so as to render it effective and capable of adequately responding to the circumstances in which it is exercised.'

b. Lay people
Speaking of the role of lay people in evangelisation par. 905 of the *Catechism of the Catholic Church*, says, 'Lay people also fulfil their prophetic mission by evangelisation, that is, the proclamation of Christ by word and the testimony of life. For lay people, this evangelisation... acquires a specific property and peculiar efficacy because it is accomplished in the ordinary circumstances of the world. This witness of life, however, is not the sole element in the apostolate; the true apostle is on the lookout for occasions of announcing Christ by word, either to unbelievers... or to the faithful.'

c. New ecclesial communities and movements
In recent years there has been growth in what are referred to as ecclesial communities and movements. Among them are Catholic Charismatic Renewal, Cursillo, Christian Life Communities, Christian Family Movement, Focolare, Schön-

statt Movement, Neo-catechumenal Way, Marriage Encounter, Communion and Liberation, the Comunità di Sant'Egidio and L'Arche. Speaking to over 300,000 members of 60 movements gathered in St. Peter's Square in 1998, Pope John Paul II said, 'You, present here, are the tangible proof of this 'outpouring' of the Spirit. Each movement is different from the others, but they are all united in the same communion and for the same mission.' He repeated what he had said in 1996 when he invited the movements to give their contribution to evangelisation through common witness and by collaborating together. He added that 'in communion with the pastors and linked with diocesan programmes,' the movements would bring 'their spiritual, educational and missionary riches to the heart of the Church as a precious experience and proposal of Christian life.'

CONCLUSION

By way of summary we conclude with some words taken from St. John Paul. In par. 3 of *Mission of the Redeemer* he wrote, 'No believer in Christ, no institution of the Church can avoid this supreme duty: to proclaim Christ to all peoples.' In par. 86 he added prophetically, 'God is preparing a great Springtime, for Christianity, and we can already see its first signs.'

Suggested questions for reflection and/or discussion

- Do you think it would be true to say that whereas faith tended to be Church centred in the past, now it is more Christ centred?

- What exactly is new about the new evangelisation?

- Who exactly are the focus of the new evangelisation?

FIVE

CONVERSION AS THE AIM OF EVANGELISATION

We are all familiar with the conversion stories of well known saints such as Paul, Augustine, and Ignatius of Loyola. The notion of conversion as acceptance of Jesus and his gospel is central in evangelisation. That is made clear in par. 46 of *Mission of the Redeemer* where John Paul II wrote, 'The proclamation of the Word of God has *Christian conversion* as its aim: a complete and sincere adherence to Christ and his Gospel through faith. Conversion is a gift of God, a work of the Blessed Trinity.'

The notion of conversion is often misunderstood insofar as it is viewed primarily as behavioural change. The Greek word for repentance, however, is *metanoia* which literally means, 'a change of mind,' i.e., in one's thinking about God which afterwards may or may not lead to a change in one's behaviour. The story of the prodigal son in Lk 15:11-32 is an outstanding example of this dynamic of change. There are three stages discernible in the parable.

- Firstly we are told that the wayward son 'came to his senses,' and decided to return to his father. In a way there was nothing particularly spiritual about this. In all probability it was a matter of expediency and enlightened self-interest. Even a life of slavery at home would be better than the miserable form of slavery he was currently enduring.

- Secondly, when the prodigal son returned home his true conversion began when he was challenged to change his thinking about his father. He acknowledged that instead of being greeted in the cold and critical way he deserved and expected, the younger son had to accept that his father greeted him in a loving and accepting way he didn't deserve. His father's non-judgmental embrace converted him from one way of thinking about his dad to another. Whereas the first stage of his conversion was occasioned by his own experience of misery, the second stage was occasioned by the revelation of the father's unconditional love. This is an important point. True conversion, as a change of behaviour is not a requirement for right relationship with God. Rather, it is a graced consequence of it.
- Thirdly, once the younger son knew what his father was really like we can presume that his behaviour began to change. The very next day he may have offered to help around the farm, not as a matter of cheerless duty, like his elder brother, but as a matter of loving conviction. His good works were not a means of earning the love and acceptance of his father, but rather gratitude for the love and acceptance he had already received as a free, unmerited gift.

POOR IN SPIRIT

In basic evangelisation, therefore, there is normally the following sequence.

Like the prodigal son, the conversion of many people begins because of an inner and outer sense of need such as:
- *Material poverty*, e.g., unemployment, lack of money, debts, poor living conditions etc.
- *Physical illness*, e.g., sickness, handicaps, injuries etc.
- *Psychological vulnerability*, e.g., addiction, depression, anxiety, stress, neurosis etc.
- *A spiritual need*, e.g., for a sense of meaning, forgiveness, love etc.

The Easter vigil liturgy refers to problems of this kind as 'happy faults' because they can become providential steppingstones to the next stage of conversion.

- The grace of conversion is the result of hearing and experiencing the Good News. As is mentioned in chapter seven, one way of encapsulating it, is to say, 'no matter what sins you have committed, if you look only into the eyes of God's mercy, expecting only mercy, you will receive only mercy, now and at the hour of your death.'
- Conversion as wholehearted trust in the unmerited gift of God's merciful love often leads to a willingness to change one's ways with the help of God. Once any of us come to know what God is like there is an implicit invitation in that experience to be for others what God is

for us. As Jesus said in Lk 6:36-38, 'Be merciful, just as your Father is merciful,' and 'love one another; even as I have loved you' (Jn 13:34). This third stage of conversion is the one when a person learns how to become a true disciple of Jesus.

CONVERSION OF CHURCHGOERS

There are many accounts of how practicing Christians have crossed the threshold of faith as a result of a conversion experience. Here is a brief account by Englishman, David Palmer who describes how he crossed the threshold from being a cultural Catholic to one who had Christ at the centre of his life.

> 'I am a Chartered Accountant and trainer and I start every course with the same words: 'I was born an Accountant and I believe in cost/benefit analysis for everything: eating, sleeping, breathing, training courses...' It's an attitude which God changed dramatically in 1996 when He became the centre of my life.
>
> I grew up in a Catholic family, was confirmed at age eight, went to a Jesuit-run secondary school and effectively left the Church at age 14 because God was irrelevant to me. I got married in a Catholic Church because my family expected me to. When I started taking my daughter to the Catholic primary school I felt it would be hypocritical not to take her to Mass. After six years of irregular Mass attendance I volunteered, so I thought, to read at Mass and become a Eucharistic Minister. A job I took seriously but

not spiritually. My faith was limited to a grudging one hour a week.

In 1996 I went on an Alpha course out of interest - much as I would have gone on a tax planning course. I soon realised that the course was about Jesus, who I had never thought of as a real person before. The revelation that He had died for me was mind-blowing. On the Holy Spirit weekend I was prayed with for the first time in my life. To experience God's love in the quiet words spoken to me was a life-changing experience.

The impact varies from the silly: previously holidays were Barcelona and Tenerife, now it's Lourdes, Celebrate at Easter and the New Dawn Conference in Walsingham; to the sacred because, I was ordained a Permanent Deacon in June 2007. My priorities have been transformed, nowadays money is no longer my reason for living.' (*GoodNews magazine*, Sept/Oct 2008).

CONVERSION OF THE UN-CHURCHED

Those engaged in the new evangelisation seek to help those who neither know the content of their faith or have an intimate relationship with Jesus as their Lord and Saviour. As Pope Benedict XVI said on Oct 7th 2012, the new evangelisation is, 'directed principally to those who, though baptised, have drifted away from the Church and live without reference to Christian life.' Here is how Marijana, a Croatian immigrant in England, described her experience.

'In my teens I had an unpleasant experience at confession and decided not to go to church any more even though we lived two minutes away from our local church... For more than 20 years it never occurred to me to go back to church or to read the Bible. I started to despise church and everything in connection with it... As life went on with its trials and tribulations I found myself three years ago not being able to get out of bed, my burden was so heavy that I could not walk straight, I had lots of mood swings, and worried about my future, work, and life in general. I did not have any happiness in my life and became very difficult in my dealings with other people.

One Sunday morning in February 2007 I woke up and had this urge to go to my local church. At the mass I felt out of place and could not wait to get out. As I left I noticed a small pink leaflet about a Life in the Spirit Seminar and decided to go there simply because it was free of charge and I did not have anything else to do that particular weekend... During the course of the seminar, to my amazement, I saw people being prayed over and dropping on the floor like flies. I overheard one lady saying that it was the best experience of her life and she would recommend everybody to be prayed over. You see, I'm a scientist by profession and to believe in anything I had to have a concrete proof and to this day I remember thinking to myself that all those people were a bit potty. So I joined the queue for prayer just to see if somebody was going to push me down on the floor. As they were praying over me

I was baptised in the Holy Spirit and since then I have never looked back.

My life has been transformed so much that my family and friends see the positive changes in me and they encourage me in my walk with Christ. On that particular Sunday in 2007 I felt that the Lord had called me by my name to show me how merciful, faithful and awesome He is, how much He loves me. I also realise that the Lord is the strength of my life, He is my Shepherd and without Him my life would be an utter mess. The Lord is the centre and focus of my life. Since 2007 I have been studying the Bible, go to church regularly... and use any opportunity to praise Him and give Him thanks for being my Abba Father and for loving me so much that He gave his one and only son for our Salvation.' (*GoodNews magazine*, Jan 2010).

CONCLUSION

It is worth pointing out that, while some Catholics experience a sudden and dramatic conversion, research indicates that for about 80% of converts it is a slow, incremental process which is not dramatic. The important thing is to come to have a committed, personal relationship with Jesus. How one gets there is of secondary importance. In Sir 5:7 we read these words, 'You should not delay being converted to the Lord, and you should not set it aside from day to day.'

SUGGESTED QUESTIONS FOR REFLECTION AND/OR DISCUSSION

- Is conversion primarily a matter of changing one's heartfelt thinking or changing one's behaviour?

- In your opinion what are the typical triggers for conversion?

- Have you ever had a conversion experience? How did it come about?

Section Three:

The Core Message

SIX

THE GOOD NEWS MESSASGE OF JESUS CHRIST

There is a very important passage in Lk 4:16-19. Let us read it first, then we can comment on it. 'He went to Nazareth, where he had been brought up, and on the Sabbath day he went into the synagogue, as was his custom. And he stood up to read. The scroll of the prophet Isaiah was handed to him. Unrolling it, he found the place where it is written: 'The Spirit of the Lord is on me, because he has anointed me to preach good news to the poor. He has sent me to proclaim freedom for the prisoners and recovery of sight for the blind, to release the oppressed, to proclaim the year of the Lord's favour.'

This was the Lord's mission statement at the beginning of his public ministry. He was describing what he intended to do. He said that he had been anointed by the Holy Spirit to bring Good News to the poor. That raises a question. Who were the poor? In his book, *New Testament Words* (London: SCM, 1971), William Barclay says that the word used in the Greek text is *ptochos*. It has three interrelated meanings. Firstly, it refers to those who have very few worldly possessions. That was the condition of the majority of the population in our Lord's time. Secondly, it refers to the down trodden and oppressed such as widows and orphans. Thirdly, it refers to those who have little or no worldly power or prestige such as servants and handicapped people. Besides having many worldly problems to contend with such as high taxes, famines, emigration, Roman cruelty and the like, the poor also had profound spiritual problems to contend with.

THE CURSE AND PENALTY OF SIN

One can get an insight into what those spiritual problems were like by reading Jn 7:48-49. It recounts how, on one occasion, the temple police had been sent to arrest Jesus who was preaching to the poor, uneducated peasants as well as many outcasts and sinners such as tax collectors, money lenders, prostitutes, and shepherds who neither knew or observed the minutiae of the Jewish law. They returned without their prisoner because they felt unwilling to bring Jesus in for questioning due to the sheer eloquence and authority of his preaching. The temple authorities said to the police, 'Has any of the rulers or of the Pharisees believed in him? No! But this mob that knows nothing of the law- *there is a curse on them.*' They said this because Deut 27:26 says, 'God's curse on anyone who does not obey all of God's laws and teachings.' Jer 11:3 endorsed that view, 'This is what the Lord, the God of Israel, says: Cursed is anyone who does not obey the terms of my covenant!' Clearly, the Jewish authorities in Jerusalem believed that the poor were cut off from God in this life and would not enter eternal life after their physical death. Furthermore they believed that the poor suffered the penalty of sin in the form of such things as sickness, disability, madness, disease, and possession by evil spirits. You may recall that when Jesus met a man who was blind from birth, 'His disciples asked him, 'Rabbi, who sinned [the curse], this man or his parents, that he was born blind [the penalty]?' (Jn 9:2). They presumed that his blindness was a penalty due to the curse of his sins or those of his parents.

THE GOOD NEWS MESSAGE OF JESUS
What was the good news that Jesus brought to the poor? Firstly, we can look at what it was not.

- It was not political. Jesus was not going to be a political and military leader like King David of old, who would take up arms against the Roman oppressors.
- It was not economic. Jesus wasn't going to bring prosperity by means of reform, investment, or social revolution.

Secondly, we can look at what his Good News was about. It was mainly spiritual in nature. Jesus intended to lift the curse of sin, and to remove its penalty. That was implied when he made his mission statement in his local synagogue in Nazareth, and said that he had been anointed 'to proclaim the year of the Lord's favour.' Let's explain what that phrase means. The Jews had a jubilee every fiftieth year. They regarded seven as the perfect number, so the year after seven sevens was the perfection of perfection. Among other things, during the jubilee year all financial debts were supposed to be cancelled.

LIFTING THE CURSE OF SIN
So when Jesus said in the beatitudes, 'blessed are the poor,' (Lk 6:20) and 'the poor in spirit,' (Mt 5:3) he was declaring a time

of spiritual jubilee when the debt of sin was being cancelled. Instead of being under a curse, as heretofore, God's unmerited mercy and love were being poured out upon the poor, free *gratis* and for nothing. All they had to do to receive it was to believe in Jesus and his gracious message. Jesus conveyed this Good News in many of his parables, e.g., the prodigal son in Lk 15: 3-31. The younger son represented the poor who failed to keep the law, and the elder son represented the Pharisees who tried to abide by the law. The younger son felt he was under a curse because he had failed to observe the law. The elder son believed that he had earned his father's favour by being dutiful and observing the law at all times. However, Jesus said that both sons were mistaken. They presumed that the father's (i.e. God's) love was conditional and had to be earned by good behaviour, whereas in actual fact it was a free, unmerited gift. Both sons were invited to the kind of conversion that leads to a change in their thinking about their father and to trust in the offer of his unconditional mercy and love. Whereas the younger son was able to change his image of his father, the elder son seemed to be unable to do so. As a result, the prodigal son entered into a new relationship with his father who clothed him with the cloak of honour, endowed him with the ring of his authority, provided him with the shoes of a beloved member of the household, and marked their new found relationship by organising a celebratory dinner. As for the elder son, who was unwilling to change his thinking about his father, he ended up in the paradoxical situation that while he was always with his father in a physical way, he ended up being alienated from him and his brother from an emotional point of view.

Removing the penalty of sin

When Jesus proclaimed his wonderful message of mercy, presumably many of the poor thought that it was too good to be true. But their doubts were dispelled when Jesus went on to remove the penalty of sin by healing and exorcising those who were brought to him. In Luke 11:20 Jesus said, 'if I drive out demons by the finger of God, then the kingdom of God has come to you.' In Mt 12:15 we read, 'Many followed him, and he healed all their sick.' There is a good example of the connection between freedom from the curse of sin and the penalty of oppressive illness in the account of a group of men who lowered their crippled friend through a hole in the roof into the presence of Jesus. We are told that, 'When Jesus saw their faith, he said to the paralytic, 'Son, your sins are forgiven' (Mark 2:5). In other words, he was telling him that the curse of his sin was being lifted from him. When the Pharisees questioned Jesus' ability to do this, he replied by saying, 'Which is easier: to say to the paralytic, 'Your sins are forgiven,' or to say, 'Get up, take your mat and walk'? But that you may know that the Son of Man has authority on earth to forgive sins [lift the curse]...' He said to the paralytic, 'I tell you, get up, take your mat and go home [removal of the penalty]' (Mk 2:9-12).

All this good news was made possible because Jesus was willing, in his great love, to become a ransom for us by acting as our scapegoat. He took the curse and penalty of sin upon himself. As scripture tells us, 'the Lord has laid on him the iniquity of us all... surely he took up our infirmities and carried our sorrows (Is 53:6; 4). As St. Paul said in 2 Cor 5:21, 'God made

Jesus who had no sin to be sin for us, so that in him we might become the righteousness of God.' Later Paul added, 'Christ redeemed us from the curse of the law by becoming a curse for us, for it is written: 'Cursed is everyone who is hung on a tree' (cf. Deut 21:23). The New Testament Church was vividly aware that as a result of Christ's saving death and resurrection, the curse of sin was lifted and that healing for the penalty of sin was available to all who believed in him and his Good News message (cf. Jm 5:13-17). As St. Peter said, 'He himself bore our sins in his body on the tree, that we might die to sin and live to righteousness. By his wounds you have been healed' (1 Pt 2:24-25).

AMAZING GRACE:
AN EXPERIENCE OF GOD'S MERCY

A few years ago I conducted a parish mission in a Dublin suburb. It was very well attended. On one of the nights I spoke about the joy of experiencing the unconditional mercy and love of Jesus. I said that it could be so vivid that it would cause tears of joy to well up. Then I asked the members of the congregation how many of them had ever wept such tears of joy. I was disappointed to find that, although there were hundreds of people in the church, only about three hands were raised. Then I said, 'my dear friends you should pray for such an awareness of the merciful love of Jesus that you will weep for joy.' About two days later I was in a counselling room in the parish centre. A woman asked me if she could talk with me. I welcomed her and said of course she could. Then she went on to recall what I had said about weeping tears of joy as a result of knowing the length and breadth the height and depth of the love of Jesus. She told me that she went home desiring that experience. 'Well Father,' she said, 'I woke up last night at about 3 a.m. weeping for joy because I was caught up in the awareness of the love of Jesus for me. I didn't want to wake up my husband so I crept out of bed, and went into an empty bedroom where I wept for joy, intermittently for about an hour.' When I heard what she said I was reminded of some words of St. Peter, 'Though you have not seen him, you love him; and even though you do not see him now, you believe in him and are filled with an inexpressible and glorious joy' (1 Pet 1:8). Clearly, the woman had experienced the liberating power of the Christian kerygma.

Conclusion

There can be little doubt that, when Jesus was evangelising, his central message was the coming of the kingdom of God. Remember how the very first words he proclaimed in Mk 1:15, were, 'The time has come,' he said. 'The kingdom of God is near. Repent and believe the good news!' What this chapter has suggested is that the phrase, 'Kingdom of God,' was an umbrella term that included the proclamation that the curse of sin was being lifted and that the penalty of sin was being removed.

Suggested Questions for Reflection and/or Discussion

1. Have you heard this Good News message of Jesus in your heart in the past?

2. Is the kerygma of Jesus preached in your church?

3. Is the good news message of Jesus one that people of today need to hear?

SEVEN

THE GOOD NEWS MESSAGE OF ST. PAUL

St. Paul was born in Tarsus in 5 A.D. In Phil 3:5, he referred to himself as being 'of the stock of Israel, of the tribe of Benjamin, a Hebrew of the Hebrews; as touching the law, a Pharisee.' In Acts 22:3 we are told that while he was still fairly young, he was sent to Jerusalem to receive his education at the school of Gamaliel, one of the most noted rabbis at the time. There he received a balanced education which included classical literature, philosophy, and ethics. When Messianic Juadism emerged, following the resurrection and ascension of Jesus, Paul, a dedicated and conscientious Pharisee, was adamantly opposed to it. In Gal 1:13 he tells us, 'For you have heard of my previous way of life in Judaism, how intensely I persecuted the church of God and tried to destroy it. I was advancing in Judaism beyond many Jews of my own age and was extremely zealous for the traditions of my fathers.'

As Acts 9:1-23; 22:6-21; 26:9-18 tell us, sometime between the years 31 and 36 A.D., Paul had a conversion experience on the way to Damascus where he intended to persecute the followers of Jesus. Up to that time he studied the law and tried to keep it. In Phil 3:5 he said, 'as for legalistic righteousness, I was faultless.' Clearly, he had attempted to be put at rights with

God by means of his good works. Before his conversion he was convinced that, unlike the mass of the Jewish people and the Gentiles, he was not under a curse like them (cf. Deut 27:26) because he had kept the law. But his views changed radically as a result of his encounter with the Risen Jesus on the road to Damascus. Three things were revealed to Paul:

- Firstly that Jesus was the promised messiah and the divine Son of God.
- Secondly, that the risen Jesus lived, by his Spirit, in the believers, who were his body on earth.
- Thirdly, he was in right relationship with God not because of anything he did, after all he had committed the sins of rejecting Jesus and persecuting his followers, but solely because of the free gift of God's grace which he had neither merited, earned or deserved. After all, he hadn't repented before his conversion by admitting his errors and seeking to change his attitudes and behaviour. Instead, God intervened suddenly and unexpectedly, and it was the revelation of Jesus' presence that changed Paul's thinking about the Messiah, his followers, and the way in which we are put at rights with God. Justification is the result of what God does and not what we do ourselves. Paul could sing with John Newton, 'Amazing grace, how sweet the sound, that saved a wretch like me. I once was lost, but now am found, was blind, but now I see.' Paul's doctrine of salvation was rooted in his conversion experience.

Paul and Jesus

In his excellent book, *The Central Message of the New Testament* (London: Fortress Press, 1981), Joachim Jeremias made the important observation that, 'It was Paul's greatness that he understood the message of Jesus as no other New Testament writer did. He was the faithful interpreter of Jesus. This is particularly true of his doctrine of justification. It was not of his own making but in substance conveys the central message of Jesus, as it is condensed in the first beatitude, 'Blessed are you poor, for yours is the kingdom of God? (Lk 6:20).' Raniero Cantalamessa, makes a similar point when he says that when St. Paul talks about justification it is a theological equivalent of Jesus talking about the coming of the kingdom. St. Paul himself acknowledged that his Gospel was derived from that of Jesus. In 1 Cor 15:3 he stated, 'For what I received I passed on to you as of first importance.'

In Rom 5:6-11 Paul explained the kerygma, 'You see, at just the right time, when we were still powerless, Christ died for the ungodly. Very rarely will anyone die for a righteous man, though for a good man someone might possibly dare to die. But God demonstrates his own love for us in this: While we were still sinners, Christ died for us. Since we have now been justified by his blood, how much more shall we be saved from God's wrath through him! For if, when we were God's enemies, we were reconciled to him through the death of his Son, how much more, having been reconciled, shall we be saved through his life!' As a result, Paul was firmly convinced that, 'a man is not justified by observing the law, but by faith in Jesus Christ. So we, too, have put our faith in Christ Jesus that we may be justified by faith in Christ and not by observing the law, because by observing the law no one will be justified' (Gal 2:16). In Eph 2:8-9 he said, 'For it is by grace you have been saved, through faith - and this not from yourselves, it is the gift of God - not by works, so that no one can boast.' Once the words of this kerygma make their home in our hearts through faith, Paul could say, 'The word is near you, in your mouth and in your heart, that is, the word of faith that we preach (i.e., the kerygma), for if you confess with your mouth, 'Jesus is Lord,' and believe in your heart that God raised him from the dead, you will be saved.' (Rm 10:8-9).

Paul believed that if a person went on to proclaim the kerygma in a Sprit-filled way, it had an inherent power to bring receptive listeners to justifying faith. In Rm 10:14, he said, 'how are men to call upon him in whom they have not believed? And how are they to believe in him of whom they have never heard? And how are they to hear without a preacher?' In Rm 10:17 he went on to assert, 'faith comes from what is heard, and what is heard comes by the preaching of Christ.' The words, 'what is heard' refer to the 'gospel' or kerygma. The phrase 'preaching of Christ' refers to anointed speech of a prophetic kind.

PROTESTANTS AND CATHOLICS ON PAULINE JUSTIFICATION

Some time ago Fr. Raniero Cantalamessa preached about the kerygma to the Pope and his household. It is interesting to see that he said in Pauline terms, 'Gratuitous justification by faith in Christ is the heart of kerygmatic preaching, and it is a shame that this in turn, is practically absent from ordinary preaching in the Church.' He went on to note that at the time of the Reformation Luther, and later other Protestant reformers, tended to say that we are justified by faith *alone*. By way of reaction Catholics insisted that without good works a person could not be justified. They rightly believed that, while one is not saved by good works, one cannot be saved without them. As Jm 2:23-24 reminds us, 'You see that a person is justified by what he does and not by faith alone.' As a result of the Reformation split however, Catholics have often failed to sufficiently emphasise the vital importance of faith in salvation, while Protestant have often failed to stress the need for good works. In 1999 this imbalance was corrected in a *Joint Declaration on Justification* which was published by the Lutheran World Federation and the Catholic Church. In Par. 15 it said, 'Together we confess: By grace alone, in faith in Christ's saving work and not because of any merit on our part, we are accepted by God and receive the Holy Spirit, who renews our hearts while equipping and calling us to good works.' Arguably, in principle if not in actual fact, that sentence puts an end to Protestantism, i.e., as the protest against the Catholic understanding of justification.

THERESE OF LISIEUX ON JUSTIFICATION

In the 19th century the French Carmelites saw themselves as willing victims of divine justice, women who took upon themselves the punishments that should rightfully have been meted out to sinners. However, in a rather Pauline way Therese put the emphasis on God's extraordinary mercy. For example she discussed this subject with an elderly companion, Sr Febronia who was near death. The latter emphasised the justice of God. Eventually Therese said to her, 'If you want divine justice, you will get divine justice. The soul gets exactly what it expects from God.' Implicit in the saint's reply, is the following principle, 'If you look into the eyes of God's mercy expecting only mercy, you will receive only mercy, now and at the hour of your death.' Either one relies on one's good works when facing God's justice, or one relies entirely on God's grace.

Therese composed the following parable in order to convey her understanding of the kerygma. 'A rabbit was eating grass in a field. Suddenly it heard the distant sounds of a bugle blowing, dogs barking and horses galloping. It looked over its shoulder in fear. It could see a king together with his courtiers out on the hunt. Clearly, they had already picked up her scent and were heading in her direction, so the rabbit took off across the fields. Eventually she ran out of energy. Soon the dogs had surrounded her. They snarled with teeth bared. They were waiting for the king, who was already dismounting, to slay the rabbit. Then they would pounce. She looked up at the king. His hand was on his sword. He was about to draw it. The rabbit thought to herself: 'If I don't do something quickly, I'm finished!' She decided to use her remaining energy to jump up onto the king's outstretched arm. So she hopped up. With eyes full of desperation and pleading she looked into the eyes of the king. When his gaze met hers something melted in his heart. His sword grip weakened. He began to stroke the rabbit with his other hand. 'I'm bringing this little creature back to the court' he said, 'My children can play with it.'

- Therese said that in this parable the rabbit is the soul.
- The dogs are our sins. They pursue us and threaten to devour us.
- The king is the Lord.
- The sword is his justice, which in justice he is entitled to use against us.
- 'But there is a fatal flaw in the heart of the king,' says Therese, 'If you expect only mercy, you will receive only mercy.'

Carmelite priest Marie-Eugene Grialou (1894-1967), who knew Therese's sisters, has suggested that her understanding of God's mercy led her to cultivate the 'art of failure.' She would intend to do some good act but would sometimes fail to do so, for one reason or another. Apparently, she would then say: 'If I had been faithful I would have received the reward of merit by appealing to God's justice. I was unfaithful, I am humiliated, I am going to receive the reward of my poverty and humiliation by appealing to God's mercy.' She believed that she would always be rewarded in times of humiliating failure by the free gift of God's merciful love. What a remarkable insight into the loving kindness of the heart of our God. It is the heartfelt conviction that her failure would inevitably call down God's blessing upon her. Is it any wonder that Eph 2:8-9 on justification by grace through faith in Jesus, was a favourite of St. Therese's.

Devotion to the divine mercy which was revealed to St. Faustina Kowalska, and advocated by her in her diaries, has strong affinities with the Pauline teaching, and that of Therese. For example, the Lord said to Faustina on one occasion, 'Souls who spread the honour of my mercy I shield through their entire lives as a tender mother her infant, and at the hour of death I will not be a Judge for them, but the Merciful Saviour. At that last hour, a soul has nothing with which to defend itself except my mercy. Happy is the soul that during its lifetime immersed itself in the Fountain of Mercy, because Justice will have no hold on it.'

SUGGESTED QUESTIONS FOR REFLECTION AND/OR DISCUSSION

1. Would you agree that although Paul uses different terminology his version of the kerygma is much the same as that of Jesus?

2. What did St. Therese of Lisieux mean when she said, 'If you want divine justice, you will get divine justice. The soul gets exactly what it expects from God.'

3. Is the teaching of St. Faustina about the mercy of God a modern version of the kerygma of St. Paul?

EIGHT

THE GOOD NEWS MESSAGE IN SIX POINTS

There is an interesting story in Acts 16:16-40. The evangelists Paul and Silas had been unjustly scourged and cast into the deepest depths of a Philippian jail and chained to the wall. Instead of complaining, they sang hymns and praised God while the other prisoners listened. We are told that as they did so there was an earthquake, their chains fell off and the doors of the prison opened. Then we read, 'When the jailer woke up and saw the prison doors wide open, he drew his sword and was about to kill himself, since he supposed that the prisoners had escaped. But Paul shouted in a loud voice, 'Do not harm yourself, for we are all here.' The jailer called for lights, and rushing in, he fell down trembling before Paul and Silas. Then he brought them outside and said, 'Sirs, what must I do to be saved?'

Let us pause here and respond to the goaler's question. 'What would you answer?' When other people have been asked this question they have given all sorts of replies such as 'believe in God,' 'Keep the commandments,' 'Live by your conscience,' 'love your neighbour as yourself,' and the like. While these answers are true up to a point, it is interesting to note what Paul and Silas actually said, 'Believe in the Lord Jesus, and you will be saved you and your household. They spoke the word of the Lord to him and to all who were in his house. At the same hour of the night he took them and washed their wounds; then he and his entire family were baptised without delay.'

When Paul and Silas said, 'Believe in the Lord Jesus,' we can presume that they would have gone on to explain what they meant. Perhaps they illustrated their point by recounting their own conversion experiences. Paul's reply raises an important question for Catholics. Are we aware that there is a hierarchy of truth, and that some truths are more basic than others? Just as a house is built on its foundations, so the Christian faith is built upon what is known as the kerygma or core Christian teaching. This raises the issue, what is that core message?

In this chapter it will be suggested that it can be divided into six basic points which spell out what is implicit in the kerygmas of Jesus and Paul. I am indepted to the Koinonia John the Baptist Community for these points. We will firstly mention what they are and then go on to describe each one in more detail.
- God loves you
- All have sinned and are in need of salvation
- Jesus died to forgive our sins
- Repent and believe
- Receive the Holy Spirit and his gifts
- Enter fully into Christian community

1. God loves you
The very first element of the Good News is not the fact of sin,

but rather that God loves you and me in an unconditional way. As Jesus said on one occasion to his disciples, 'As the Father loves me, so I love you. Now remain in my love' (Jn 15:9). God's infinite love for his divine and sinless son is wholly deserved. However, what is truly amazing is the fact that Jesus has the same love for us as creatures, and sinful ones at that. Knowing how important this awareness was, St Paul said, 'I pray that you, being rooted and established in love, may have power, together with all the saints, to grasp how wide and long and high and deep is the love of Christ, and to know this love that surpasses knowledge-that you may be filled to the measure of all the fullness of God' (Eph 3:17-19).

2. All have sinned and are in need of salvation

Our sins prevent us from fully experiencing the presence and the love of God. The Greek word for sin literally means 'to miss the mark,' such as happens when an arrow fails to hit the target. God expects us to lead loving lives, by obeying the commandments, especially the great commandment of loving our neighbours as ourselves. However, the good we wish to do, we sometimes fail to do, and the evil we wish to avoid is exactly what we do, as a result of either weakness or malice. That is why St. Paul said, 'the scriptures declare that the whole world is a prisoner of sin' (Gal 3:22). So he could declare, 'All have sinned and fall short of the glory of God,' (Rom 3:23-24). St. John added, 'If we claim we have not sinned, we make God out to be a liar and his word has no place in our lives' (1 Jn 1:10). Many people nowadays are unaware of their sins. However God can reveal the dust of sin as an absence of love by the light of divine love. As the scripture says, 'You rebuke offenders little by little, warn them and remind them of the sins they are committing' (Wis 12:2).

3. Jesus died to forgive our sins

When Jesus proclaimed, 'Blessed are the poor, the Kingdom of God is yours' (Lk 6:20), he was declaring that through no merit or good work on their part, the curse of sin was being lifted from those who acknowledged their need for the free gift of God's merciful love which was being poured out upon them. As we saw in the chapter on the kerygma of Jesus, this was made possible because Jesus, as our scapegoat, took the curse of sin upon himself. We are reminded of this amazing truth at every mass we attend. For example, at the consecration of the wine, the priest says, 'Take this, all of you, and drink from it: this is the cup of my blood, the blood of the new and everlasting covenant. It will be shed for you and for many *so that sins may be forgiven.*'

4. Repent and believe

Many of us find it hard to acknowledge our failings which tend to blind us and prevent us from seeing who God really is. Pride can make us reluctant to honestly admit them without excusing or minimising them, e.g., by attributing them to impersonal factors such as environmental pressures, unconscious influences, addictive tendencies etc. Like the Prodigal Son we need to come to our senses by opening the eyes of our hearts to the revelation of who Jesus is and how great is his divine mercy and love, in such a way that we change our thinking about God, acknowledge our wrongdoings and trust in the Lord's endless goodness for our justification, rather than in any merit of our own.

One way of repenting is to say this prayer in a sincere way, 'Lord, Jesus, I come before You, just as I am. I am sorry for my sins, I repent of them, please forgive me. In Your name, I forgive all others for what they have done against me. I renounce Satan, the evil spirits and all their works. I give You my entire self. Lord Jesus, now and forever, I invite You into my life. I accept You as my Lord and Saviour. Heal me, change me, strengthen me in body, soul and spirit. Come Lord Jesus, cover me with Your precious blood, and fill me with Your Holy Spirit, I love You Jesus. I praise You Jesus. I thank You Jesus. I shall follow You every day of my life. Amen.'

5. Receive the Holy Spirit and his gifts
St. Paul wrote, 'Be filled with the Spirit' (Eph 5:18). Rather than being advice, this is a command of the Lord. Without the Spirit we can do nothing, but when the Spirit who is the Lord and Giver of Life is active within us, we can do all things. To receive the Holy Spirit and his gifts, we simply need to ask with expectant faith, relying on Jesus' promise: 'If you then, though you are evil, know how to give good gifts to your children, how much more will your Father in heaven give the Holy Spirit to those who ask him!' (Lk 11:13). For more on this see chapter nine.

As we ask for the Holy Spirit, we should be open to receiving his gifts, those outlined in Is 11:2 and 1 Cor 12:8-10. In Is 11:2 we read, 'The spirit of the Lord shall rest upon him: a spirit of wisdom and of understanding, a spirit of counsel and of strength, a spirit of knowledge and fear of the Lord.' In 1 Cor 12:8-10 we read, 'To one is given through the Spirit the expression of wisdom; to another the expression of knowledge according to the same Spirit; to another faith by the same Spirit; to another gifts of healing by the same Spirit; to another mighty deeds; to another prophecy; to another discernment of spirits; to another varieties of tongues; to another interpretation of tongues.' These charismatic gifts are expressions of the love of God and help us to build up a loving Christian community. As par. 12 of the *Constitution on the Church* says, 'These charismatic gifts are to be received with thanksgiving for they are exceedingly suitable and useful for the needs of the Church.' We will return to this subject in chapter ten.

6. Enter into the Christian community
When people accept the kerygma they will need to find a group who will support them in their new life of faith, e.g., a Prayer Group, Parish Cell or Bible Study Group that meets regularly. This was the way of life in the early church. As St. Luke tells us, 'They devoted themselves to the apostles' teaching and to the fellowship, to the breaking of bread and to prayer. And the Lord added to their community daily those who were being saved' (Acts 2:42, 47). Paul calls this community the Body of Christ. We are the gifted members of that Body and Jesus is our head. It is almost impossible to grow to be a true disciple of Christ without the help and nurturance of a loving community, giving us a

sense of belonging and practical support, and building up our faith through teaching, thereby helping us to resist the false values of secular society and thereby grow in holiness of life.

Conclusion

It is good for evangelisers to have the six points of the kerygma in mind as they evangelise. By the way, Fr. Jonathan Cotton has written a book on the subject entitled, *Evangelising the Baptised: The First Six Steps for Catholics Towards a New Evangelisation* (Luton: New Life, 2014). That said, evangelisers should avoid using the six points in a rigid inflexible way. As Pope Francis warns in par. 129 of *The Joy of the Gospel*, 'We should not think, however, that the Gospel message must always be communicated by fixed formulations learned by heart or by specific words which express an absolutely invariable content.'

Suggested questions for reflection and/or discussion

- Why do you think that instead of focusing first and foremost on the universal reality of sin, the kerygma of the early church, focused instead on the unconditional love of God?

- Do you think that Pope Francis was correct when he said, 'We should not think, however, that the Gospel message must always be communicated by fixed formulations.'

- Because of a lack of awareness of the person of God, many people nowadays are not really aware of personal sin. Who or what will help them become aware of the ways in which they have fallen short of the glory of God?

Section Four:

Power for the New Evangelisation

NINE

THE HOLY SPIRIT AND THE NEW EVANGELISATION

It is striking that Jesus, and his mother Mary, received an in-filling of the Spirit before they began to evangelise. The Spirit was not given to make them holy. They were that already. It was given to equip them to evangelise in power.

Knowing this to be true Pope John XXIII prayed at the inauguration of Vatican II, 'O Holy Spirit, renew your wonders in this our day, as by a new Pentecost.' Years later Pope John Paul II echoed that prayer when he wrote in par. 21 of *Mission of the Redeemer*, 'The Holy Spirit is indeed the principle agent of the whole of the Church's mission... Through his action the Good News takes shape in human minds and hearts and extends through history. In all of this it is the Holy Spirit who gives life.'

Recent Popes have all insisted that effective evangelisation is not possible without the help of the Holy Spirit.

- Pope Paul VI said in par. 76 of *Evangelisation in the Modern World*, 'Evangelisation will never be possible without the action of the Holy Spirit... Techniques of evangelisation are good, but even the most advanced ones could not replace the gentle action of the Spirit. The most perfect preparation of the evangeliser has no effect without the Holy Spirit... Without Him the most highly developed schemas resting on a sociological or psychological basis are quickly seen to be quite valueless.'

- In par. 87 of *Mission of the Redeemer*, Pope John Paul II wrote, 'a life of complete docility to the Spirit commits us to being moulded from within by the Spirit, so that we may become ever more like Christ. It is not possible to bear witness to Christ without reflecting his image, which is made alive in us by grace and the power of the Spirit.'
- Pope Benedict said at a mass in 2012, 'Paul leaves us a very valuable teaching, taken from his experience. He writes: 'our gospel came to you not only in word, but also in power and in the Holy Spirit and with full conviction.' Evangelisation, to be effective, needs the power of the Spirit, who gives life to proclamation and imbues those who convey it with the 'full conviction' of which the Apostle speaks.'
- Pope Francis also highlights the role of the Holy Spirit in evangelisation. For instance in par. 261 of *The Joy of the Gospel* he says, 'A spirit-filled evangelisation is one guided by the Holy Spirit, for he is the soul of the Church called to proclaim the Gospel.'

THINGS GO WRONG AFTER VATICAN II

Those of us who are old enough to remember the Second Vatican Council will recall the great optimism there was when it concluded. We had wonderful blueprints for change in the liturgy, relationships with other Christian churches, and with the modern world. It was not long however before divisions and disillusionment set in. Tens of thousands of priests and nuns left their vocations and the numbers joining seminaries fell. Following the publication of *On the Regulation of Birth* (1968), which banned all forms of artificial contraception, millions of lay people dissented from what the Church taught.

ANTECEDENTS TO BLESSING

On February 17th 1967, a few years after the conclusion of the Council, twenty five students from Duquesne University attended a momentous retreat in The Ark and the Dove Retreat House on the outskirts of the city. Kevin and Dorothy Ranaghan have described their state of mind in this way, 'There was something lacking in their individual Christian lives. They couldn't quite put their finger on it, but somehow there was an emptiness, a lack of dynamism, a sapping of strength in their lives of prayer and action. It was as if their lives as Christians were too much their own creation, as if they were moving forward under their own power and of their own will. It seemed to them that the Christian life wasn't meant to be a purely human achievement.' Each of the people who attended the retreat read David Wilkerson's *The Cross and the Switchblade*, the first four chapters of the *Acts of the Apostles*, and asked for a new outpouring of the Holy Spirit. Afterwards they claimed to have experienced a powerful release of the Spirit and his charismatic gifts.

Patti Mansfield has described her experience of what happened to her during the retreat in these moving words. 'I wandered into the upstairs chapel... not to pray but to tell any students there to come down to the (birthday) party. Yet, when I entered and knelt in the presence of Jesus in the Blessed Sacrament, I literally trembled with a sense of awe before His majesty. I knew in an overwhelming way that He is the King of Kings, the Lord of Lords. I thought, 'You had better get out of here quickly before something happens to you.' But overriding my fear was a much greater desire to surrender myself unconditionally to God. I prayed, 'Father, I give my life to you. Whatever you ask of me, I accept. And if it means suffering, I accept that too. Just teach me to follow Jesus and to love as He loves.' In the next moment, I found myself prostrate, flat on my face, and flooded with an experience of the merciful love of God... a love that is totally undeserved, yet lavishly given. Yes, it's true what St. Paul writes, 'The love of God has been poured into our hearts by the Holy Spirit.' My shoes came off in the process. I was indeed on holy ground. I felt as if I wanted to die and be with God. The prayer of St. Augustine captured my experience: 'O Lord, you have made us for yourself and our hearts are restless until they rest in You.' As much as I wanted to bask in His presence, I knew that if I, who am no one special, could experience the love of God in this way, then anyone across the face of the earth could do so.'

BE FILLED WITH THE SPIRIT
What Patti Mansfield experienced is what is referred to as baptism or the infilling of the Spirit. The word baptism in English comes from Greek and means 'to immerse,' i.e., to soak, inundate, or saturate. In other words, to be baptised in the

Spirit, means to be drenched with the Spirit (cf. Eph 5:18). As Jn 1:33 shows, there is nothing new about the phrase 'baptised in the Spirit.' It is significant that Jesus used a similar phrase before his ascension into heaven when he said to the apostles, 'John baptised with water, but in a few days you will be baptised with the Holy Spirit' (Acts 1:5). This promise was fulfilled with the outpouring of the Spirit at Pentecost.

In 2012 the Doctrinal Commission of the International, Catholic, Charismatic Renewal Services published a short, but important book entitled, *Baptism in the Holy Spirit* (Luton: New Life, 2012). It argues that a Pentecostal in-filling of the Spirit is *integral* to the sacraments of baptism and confirmation, and *normative* for all Christians. Baptism in the Spirit is both a *release* of the grace we received in a sacramental way when we were baptised and confirmed, and also a *reception* of charisms which are useful for effective evangelisation. In an important definition the book states that, 'Baptism in the Spirit is a life-transforming experience of the love of God the Father poured into one's heart by the Holy Spirit, and received through a total surrender to the lordship of Jesus Christ. This grace brings alive sacramental baptism and confirmation, deepens communion with God and with fellow Christians, enkindles evangelistic fervour and equips a person with charisms for service and mission.' Is it any wonder, therefore, that Pope Benedict XVI said, 'let us rediscover, dear brothers and sisters, the beauty of being baptised in the Holy Spirit; let us recover awareness of our Baptism and our Confirmation, ever timely sources of grace.' To experience baptism in the spirit does not necessarily mean that the recipient has joined a movement, any movement. Rather it is an appropriation of the fullness of Christian initiation, which belongs to the church. It is, above all else, an empowerment for evangelisation.

RECEIVING THE IN-FILLING OF THE SPIRIT

How does a person become baptised in the Holy Spirit? In my experience, four things are necessary.

Firstly, he or she needs a wholehearted *desire* for this grace. Sometimes it takes months and even years for the desire to deepen and strengthen to such a point that the personality is sufficiently open to receive the un-merited gift of the outpouring of the Spirit.

Secondly, it is important to rely on the infallible *promises of God* to send the Spirit to those, whose desire prompts them to ask for it. Here is just one of many possible New Testament examples. In Lk 11:13, Jesus said to parents, 'If you then, though you are evil, know how to give good gifts to your children, how much more will your Father in heaven give the Holy Spirit to those who ask him!' As Catholics, we pray to Mary, the mother of Jesus, to be worthy of this mighty promise of Christ.

Thirdly, it is important that those who desire to be filled with the Spirit would be willing to *turn away from any obstacle* that might stand in the way. While all un-repented sin is a barrier, in my experience the greatest single obstacle is resentment, an unwillingness to forgive past hurts and injustices whether real or imaginary. Incidentally, scripture seems to confirm that impression, for example in Mk 11:24-25; Lk 6:36-38. So it is necessary for those who want to be baptised in the Spirit to prepare by being willing, with God's help, to turn away from sin, especially, the sin of anger and antagonism against any person living or dead.

Fourthly, people should *ask* to be baptised in the Spirit with real expectancy. There are many gifts we could ask for from God, without being certain that they are in accord with the divine will. But to ask to be filled with the Holy Spirit is always in accord with the centrality of God's plan for us. As scripture assures us: 'This is the confidence we have in approaching God: that if we ask anything according to his will, he hears us. And if we know that he hears us - whatever we ask - we know that we have what we asked of him' (1 Jn 5:14-15). As soon as people begin to ask for the sending of the Spirit, they receive a first instalment of that grace. At the outset they may not be consciously aware of any inner change. But then, either suddenly or gradually, their relationship with Christ will deepen as a result of a religious awakening.

If you desire an in-filling of the Holy Spirit, say the following prayer with sincerity of heart and expectant trust, 'Lord Jesus Christ, I want to belong more fully to you from this time forward. I want to be freed from the power of sin and the evil one. I will turn away from all wrongdoing, and I will avoid everything that leads me to wrongdoing. I ask you to forgive all the sins that I have committed. I offer my life to you, and I promise to put you first and to seek to do your will. I ask you now to drench, soak, and inundate me with your Holy Spirit. I believe that your spiritual hands are upon me and that the red light of your mercy and the white light of your love are flooding my body, mind and soul. I thank you Lord that even as I pray you are responding to my request because it is so in accord with your loving desire for me.'

Conclusion

A booklet entitled *Fanning the Flame* (Collegeville: Liturgical Press, 1991), observes, 'accepting the baptism in the Spirit is not joining a movement, any movement.' In another place McDonnell and Montague added: 'The baptism in the Holy Spirit does not belong to private piety... *it is the spirituality of the church* [my italics].' Because it is so clearly associated with the sacraments of initiation, a concerted effort is needed, when preparing candidates for baptism and confirmation, e.g., during RCIA courses, to encourage them to expect the Holy Spirit to come upon them with such power that they will receive, not only the gifts mentioned in Is 11:2, but also those mentioned in 1 Cor 12:8-10. Empowered by the Spirit and his gifts, Catholics will be enabled, by means of the new evangelisation, to bring about the new Springtime spoken about by Pope John Paul II, in par. 86 of *Mission of the Redeemer*.

Suggested questions for reflection and/or discussion

- When Pope John XXIII prayed for a new Pentecost in the Church, what do you think he had in mind?

- If he knew that we received the Holy Spirit in baptism and confirmation, why would St. Paul say to us, 'be filled with the Spirit' (Eph 5:18).

- Why is the Holy Spirit so important where evangelisation is concerned?

TEN

THE GIFTS OF THE SPIRIT AND EVANGELISATION

Following his baptism at the Jordan, Jesus did two main things. Acts 1:1 says that he began to do and to teach. In other words he *proclaimed* the Good News of God's unconditional mercy and love, especially to the poor, and he *demonstrated* the reality of that Good News, especially by means of healings, exorcisms and miracles. When he proclaimed the Good News he announced the fact that the curse of sin was being lifted. As we saw in chapter six, the Jews believed that illness and handicaps were the penalty of sin. So as a sign that the curse of sin had indeed been lifted, Jesus removed the penalty of sin as well, by healing the sick and driving out evil spirits.

THE COMMISSION TO PROCLAIM AND DEMONSTRATE THE GOOD NEWS

During his lifetime Jesus instructed the apostles to do the same. Like him, they were to proclaim and demonstrate the coming of the Kingdom of God. In Jn 14:12 Jesus promised, 'I tell you the truth, anyone who has faith in me will do what I have been doing. He will do even greater things than these, because I am going to the Father.' In Mk 16:15-19 we read: 'He said to them, 'Go into all the world and preach the good news to all creation.

Whoever believes and is baptised will be saved, but whoever does not believe will be condemned. And these signs will accompany those who believe: In my name they will drive out demons... they will place their hands on sick people, and they will get well.' There is clear evidence in the Acts and especially the earlier epistles of Paul, that the apostles did carry out the Lord's instructions. They not only proclaimed the Good News, they demonstrated it in deeds of power. As Acts 2:43 testifies, 'Many wonders and signs were done through the apostles.' In Acts 14:3-4 we are told that, 'Paul and Barnabas spent considerable time (in Iconium), speaking boldly for the Lord, who confirmed the message of his grace by enabling them to do miraculous signs and wonders.'

There is clear evidence that the charisms were exercised in early Christianity. However, for a number of reasons they began to die out during the first three centuries. The emphasis shifted to the institutional church, its sacraments and rituals as means of grace. Priests and people expected the Spirit to be manifested by the witness of lives well lived and in action for justice and deeds of mercy, but not by unusual charismatic activity. St. Thomas Aquinas taught that canonisable saints were the only exception to this rule during their lifetimes and after their deaths. He wrote, 'True miracles cannot be wrought save by the power of God, because God works them... in proof of a person's holiness which God desires to propose as an example of virtue.'

Charismatic Revival at Vatican II

For Catholics, all this began to change at the Second Vatican Council. In par. 12 of the *Constitution on the Church* and par. 3 of the Decree on the Laity, the pope and bishops made ten important points to do with the more unusual charisms.

1. Grace comes to us primarily through sacraments and clerical ministry.
2. Grace also comes through the gifts of the Spirit in general, and the charisms mentioned in Rm 12:6-8; Eph 4:4 and Cor 12: 8-10 in particular.
3. The Holy Spirit distributes what are variously referred to as 'simple' and 'exceptional' gifts, among lay people.
4. These gifts are given to build up the Church in holiness and to develop people.
5. The charisms are a wonderful means of apostolic vitality.
6. These gifts are to be received with gratitude and consolation.
7. People, whether clerical or lay have a right to exercise their charisms and ministries. This right comes from their baptism and not from the clergy.
8. Lay people have a duty to use their charisms for the good of the Church and the world.
9. Bishops and clergy should test the charisms to see that they are genuine and used for the common good.
10. However, the clergy should be careful not to quench the Spirit by an arbitrary use of authority.

Classification of the Charisms

Paul's theology of the gifts is an expression of his awareness, not of his reading. So when he listed the charisms in 1 Cor 12:8-10, he probably did so in the light of his personal experience of evangelisation. Following St. Thomas Aquinas I would suggest, however, that they can be classified in the following way:

- There are charisms of *revelation* that enable the believer to know the presence, word and will of the Lord, e.g., wisdom, knowledge, prophetic revelation, words of knowledge.
- There are charisms of *proclamation* that enable the believer to preach, teach or share the Good News, e.g., utterance of words of wisdom and knowledge, prophecy proclaimed..
- There are charisms of *demonstration* which manifest the Good news, e.g., by means of liberating deeds of power such as faith, healings and miracle working.

This is a quasi-sacramental view, where word and deed, together conspire to make the risen Christ present.

CHARISMS AND PROCLAIMING THE GOOD NEWS

Sadly, we are living at a time when millions of Europeans have drifted away from the Church. Many of them have little or no sense of a supernatural realm beyond sense experience. When Christians can demonstrate the truth of the Good News message by means of supernatural deeds of power, such as healings and miracles, they manifest the power and presence of the risen Lord. As Nicodemus said to Jesus, 'Rabbi, we know that you are a teacher come from God, for no one can do these signs that you do unless God is with him' (Jn 3:2). Jesus himself said, 'Do not believe me unless I do what my Father does. But if I do it, even though you do not believe me, believe the miracles' (Jn 10:37-38).

In 1974, when Pope Paul VI was launching Cardinal Suenen's book, *A New Pentecost?* (London: DLT, 1975), he said in the course of some impromptu remarks, 'How wonderful it would be if the Lord would again pour out the charisms in increased abundance, in order to make the Church fruitful, beautiful and marvelous, and to enable it to win the attention and astonishment of the profane and secularised world.' In an article entitled, 'The Charisms and the New Evangelisation' which was published in *GoodNews* magazine (Jan/Feb 2007), Cardinal Danneels echoed those sentiments when he wrote, 'In times of crisis like today, the Spirit multiplies its gifts.' A little later he added, 'The more the life of the people of God is harsh, the more God grants his gifts. What would be the particular gifts today which the Lord gives us? Would it not be faith which moves mountains, which brings about miracles and which thus gives weight to the proclamation of the gospel?'

Pope Benedict XVI wrote a letter to priests in 2009 to celebrate the 150th anniversary of the birth of St. John Vianney, in the course of which he said that the 'varied charismatic gifts of the laity,... which awaken in many people the desire for a deeper spiritual life... can provide, a helpful impulse to a renewed commitment by the Church in proclaiming and bearing witness to the Gospel of hope and charity in every corner of the world.'

In 2012, proposition 43 of the post-synodal document *The New Evangelisation for the Transmission of the Christian Faith* stated, 'The hierarchical gifts and the charismatic gifts, flowing from the one Spirit of God, are not in competition but rather co-essential to the life of the Church and to the effectiveness of her missionary action.' Sometime later Pope Francis talked about the role of the charisms in par. 130 of *The Joy of the Gospel* when he wrote, 'They are not an inheritance, safely secured and entrusted to a small group for safekeeping [e. g. the members of the Charismatic Renewal], rather they are gifts of the Spirit integrated into the body of the Church, drawn to the centre which is Christ and then channeled into *an evangelising impulse* (my italics).'

CONCLUSION

Mention of the charismatic gifts in the documents of Vatican II has proven to be truly prophetic. From 1967 onwards the Lord has poured them out on the clergy and laity alike. Fifty years after the ending of the Council, well over 100 million Catholics have been baptised in the Spirit, and received the gifts mentioned in 1 Cor 12:8-10. Commenting on this phenomenon, Pope Benedict XVI has said, 'In the heart of a world adversely affected by rationalistic skepticism, a new experience of the Holy Spirit has come about, amounting to a worldwide renewal movement. What the New Testament describes with reference to the charisms as visible signs of the coming of the Spirit is no longer merely ancient, past history: this history is becoming a burning reality today.' We end this chapter with some words spoken by St. John Paul II at Pentecost 1998, at an historical gathering of new ecclesial movements and communities in Rome, 'Today, I would like to cry out to all of you gathered here in St. Peter's Square and to all Christians: Open yourselves docilely to the gifts of the Spirit! Accept gracefully and obediently the charisms which the Spirit never ceases to bestow on us! Do not forget that every charism is given for the common good, that is, for the benefit of the whole Church.' Amen to that!

Suggested Questions for Reflection and/or Discussion

- When we were being confirmed we were told about the gifts of the Holy Spirit which are mentioned in Is 11:2, 'the Spirit of wisdom and of understanding, the Spirit of counsel and of power, the Spirit of knowledge and of the fear of the Lord.' How come the more specifically Christian gifts mentioned in 1 Cor 12: 8-10 were not mentioned?

- Do you agree with the view of Cardinal Danneels that the charisms are being restored to help people in our secular culture to believe in Jesus?

- Are you open to receive whatever ordinary or extraordinary gifts the Lord might want to give you in order to evangelise effectively?

ELEVEN

THE WORD OF GOD AND EVANGELISATION

In *The Joy of the Gospel*, Pope Francis said in par 174, 'The sacred Scriptures are the very source of evangelisation. Consequently, we need to be constantly trained in hearing the word. The Church does not evangelise unless she constantly lets herself be evangelised. It is indispensable that the word of God 'be ever more fully at the heart of every ecclesial activity.' God's word, listened to and celebrated, above all in the Eucharist, nourishes and inwardly strengthens Christians, enabling them to offer an authentic witness to the Gospel in daily life.' In par. 175 he said, 'The study of the sacred Scriptures must be a door opened to every believer. It is essential that the revealed word radically enrich our catechesis and all our efforts to pass on the faith. Evangelisation demands familiarity with God's word, which calls for dioceses, parishes and Catholic associations to provide for a serious, ongoing study of the Bible, while encouraging its prayerful individual and communal reading.'

God's Word as an abstract Noun and a living Verb

The word of God can be viewed as a noun or a verb. As a noun it is objectively true upon the page. As such it can be studied and interpreted in an academic way. As a verb that is spoken to the heart, the word of God can become subjectively true, at a particular time, in a particular circumstance, for a particular individual/s.

There is a story in the first Book of Samuel which illustrates the difference between the word of God as a noun and a verb. We are told that the young Samuel, 'did not yet know the Lord: The word of the Lord had not yet been revealed to him' (1 Sam 3:7). What the inspired author seems to be saying is that, while Samuel was familiar with the word of God as a noun, he had not yet heard the word as a verb spoken to his heart. When he was repeatedly woken by the Lord during the night 'Eli [the priest] realised that God was calling the boy. So he told Samuel, 'Go and lie down, and if God calls you, say, 'Speak, Lord, for your servant is listening" (1 Sam 3:8-9).

The possibility of receiving and sharing revelation in this way is referred to in a number of places in the Old Testament. Here are just two examples, 'Call to me and I will answer you and tell you great and unsearchable things you do not know' (Jer 33:3), and 'From now on I will tell you of new things, of hidden things unknown to you. They are created now, and not long ago; you have not heard of them before today. So you cannot say, 'Yes, I knew of them.' (Is 48:6-7).

LECTIO DIVINA
St. Augustine once said: 'He is undoubtedly barren who preaches outwardly the word of God without hearing it

inwardly.' So it is not surprising that in Par. 25 of the *Dogmatic Constitution on Divine Revelation* we read, 'Prayer should accompany the reading of Sacred Scripture, so that God and human beings may talk together; for we speak to him when we pray; *we hear him when we read the divine sayings.*'

The Catholic Church encourages its members and especially evangelisers to engage in regular periods of *lectio divina* (i.e. Divine reading), as a traditional, yet fruitful way of reading and praying the scriptures. For example, in par. 152 of *The Joy of the Gospel* Pope Francis wrote, 'There is one particular way of listening to what the Lord wishes to tell us in his word and of letting ourselves be transformed by the Spirit. It is what we call *lectio divina*. It consists of reading God's word in a moment of prayer and allowing it to enlighten and renew us.' By the Spirit's help, this way of praying enables the word upon the page, to become a living word that is spoken to the heart.

1. Petition
One begins with a petition for divine guidance. *Evangelise Today: Sharing the Good News of Jesus Christ*, which was published by the Irish Episcopal Conference, contains the following prayer, 'Compassionate God, anoint me with your Holy Spirit, as I read your Word, and let me hear your voice speaking to me within. May your word be the joy of my heart and a lamp for my steps. I desire to build my life on your word. Give me the wisdom to understand what you are saying to me. May I rejoice in the blessedness of hearing your word and keeping it. Speak Lord your servant is listening.'

2. Read

One goes on to read a chosen text and seeks to discover what the inspired author intended to say. Without this kind of objective approach, there is always a risk that one interprets the text in terms of one's own preconceived ideas. Speaking about this possibility Pope Francis said in par. 152 of *The Joy of the Gospel*, 'The spiritual reading of a text must start with its literal sense. Otherwise we can easily make the text say what we think is convenient, useful for confirming us in our previous decisions, suited to our own patterns of thought.' To this end many Christians find that it is useful to have access to a study Bible with lots of explanatory footnotes or a good scripture commentary.

3. Meditate

Next comes meditation, which asks: what does the biblical text say to me, and what relevance has it in today's world? In par. 153 of *The Joy of the Gospel* Pope Francis proposes that the praying person ask the following questions, 'Lord, what does this text say to me? What is it about my life that you want to change by this text? What troubles me about this text? Why am I not interested in this? Or perhaps: What do I find pleasant in this text? What is it about this word that moves me? What attracts me? Why does it attract me?' Here, each person individually, but also as a member of the community, must let himself or herself be moved and challenged.'

4. Pray

Prayer follows. As the person ponders God's word it evokes all kinds of inner reactions, feelings and desires. It is important to tell God about them a prayerful way. As Luther said, 'prayer is not telling lies to God.' It requires us to tell the truth, the whole truth and nothing but the truth about our subjective response to the text.

5. Contemplate

Lectio divina concludes with contemplation, during which the word of God as a noun on the page can leap alive and active off the page into the heart as the spoken word of God which is true for the hearer right now. It can reveal the Person, word and will of God.

An important discipline which aids contemplation is the ability to quieten the body and mind. When I am praying I try to sit with my back straight and my arms either folded or resting gently on my knees. Once I have assumed my prayer pose I try to remain completely still during the contemplative period of my prayer time without moving a muscle. This usually lasts for ten to fifteen minutes. I find that if my body is quiet, my mind also tends to become quiet. I also seek to control my thoughts so as to be in a state of silent receptivity. During this time I can receive inspirations, promptings and revelations. It might be a scripture text, something that occurred to me during the last day or two, or an idea I pondered in a prayerful way on a previous occasion. It could be a spontaneous mental picture, an inner vision, an inner voice, a sudden intellectual awareness.

Pope John Paul II stated in par. 91 of *The Mission of the Redeemer*,

'The missionary must be a 'contemplative in action.' He or she finds answers to problems in the light of God's word and in personal and community prayer... the future of mission depends to a great extent on contemplation. Unless the missionary is a contemplative he or she cannot proclaim Christ in a credible way. He is a witness to the experience of God, and must be able to say with the apostles: 'that which we have looked upon... concerning the word of life... we proclaim also to you' (1 Jn 1:1-3).' On another occasion Pope John Paul II said to The Catholic Fraternity of Covenant Communities and Fellowships (2001), 'Contemplation which does not give life to mission is condemned to frustration and failure... because contemplation engenders evangelisation.'

6. Resolution

Lastly, one does well to remember that the process of *lectio divina* is not fully concluded until it leads the praying person/s to make a practical resolution which will help him or her to express in action what the Lord has revealed. Ideally it should be single, precise and possible.

CONCLUSION

As I have engaged in regular lectio divina over the years, like so many others, I have not only grown in knowledge of God in and through the scriptures, I have also received the inspirations that have informed my evangelisation. As Pope Francis warned in par 151 of *The Joy of the Gospel*, if an evangelist, 'does not take time to hear God's word with an open heart, if he does not allow it to touch his life, to challenge him, to impel him, and if he does not devote time to pray with that word, then he will indeed be a false prophet, a fraud, a shallow impostor.'

Suggested Questions for Reflection and/or Discussion

- Would you agree that prayerful reflection on the scriptures is the very source of effective evangelisation? If so why?

- Pope Francis has said, that the person who does not devote time to pray with the word, will 'be a false prophet, a fraud, a shallow impostor.' What do you think he means by that assertion?

- What does lectio divina mean by the word contemplation? Why did John Paul II think that contemplation and evangelisation are inextricably linked?

TWELVE

COMMUNITY AND EVANGELISATION

New Testament Christians believed that there was a close connection between friendship in the community and effective evangelisation. St. Luke described the link in three passages; Acts 2:42-47; 5:12-15; and especially 4:32-36 which reads: 'All the believers were one in heart and mind. No one claimed that any of his possessions was his own, but they shared everything they had. With great power the apostles continued to testify to the resurrection of the Lord Jesus, and much grace was upon them all. There were no needy persons among them. For from time to time those who owned lands or houses sold them, brought the money from the sales and put it at the apostle's feet, and it was distributed to anyone as he had need.'

A number of comments can be made about these verses. Firstly, the opening one echoes the teaching of the Greeks, Jews and Romans on the nature of friendship. For example, in the 5th century B.C. Pythagoras founded a community of friends. It had four guidelines, the first two which were, 'Friends share in the perfect communion of a single spirit, friends share everything in common.' It would probably be accurate to say that Luke was consciously and deliberately saying that, thanks to the transforming power of grace, the early Christians fulfilled these ancient ideals of friendship, i.e., unity of mind and heart expressed in a sharing of goods. Although some members of the early Christian church may have been intimate friends, I don't think that Luke was implying that all the members were necessarily sharing their inmost thoughts and feelings with one another. They were one in mind and heart in so far as they were conformed to the mind and heart of Christ. St. Paul seemed to endorse this interpretation when he said:

- In Phil 2:2, 'Be of the same mind, having the same love, being in full accord and of one mind… Let the same mind be in you that was in Christ'.
- In Romans 15:5-6 he said 'May the God who gives endurance and encouragement give you a spirit of unity among yourselves as you follow Christ Jesus so that with one heart and mouth you may glorify the God and Father of our Lord Jesus Christ'
- In 1 Cor 1:10 he said 'Finally, all of you, live in harmony with one another; be sympathetic, love as brothers and sisters, be compassionate and humble'.

What is really significant in the passage, adverted to in Acts 4: 32-36 is the fact that Luke inserted a verse about evangelisation into the middle of a passage on community relationships, i.e., 'With great power the apostles continued to testify to the resurrection of the Lord Jesus, and much grace was upon them.' What he seemed to be saying was this; friendly, loving relationships in the community energise effective evangelisation, while being a living icon of that Good News.

In par. 32 of *On the Vocation and Mission of the Laity in the Church*, St. John Paul II endorsed this scriptural point of view when he wrote, 'Communion and mission are profoundly connected with each other, they interpenetrate and mutually imply each other, to the point that communion represents both the source and the fruit of mission: communion gives rise to mission and mission is accomplished in communion. It is always the one and the same Spirit who calls together and unifies the Church and sends her to preach the Gospel 'to the ends of the earth' (Acts 1:8).'

A MEMORABLE EXPERIENCE

Many years ago I belonged to a prayer group in the North of Ireland. At one point about sixteen of the more experienced members felt led, after a good deal of prayerful discernment, to form a sort of community. At our very first get-together I gave a talk on Christian community as a network of friendships. When I invited comments, a number of people said that they thought that the ideal I had proposed was too demanding. We prayed for a while. Then one of the members, a lorry driver, got a remarkable inspiration. Spontaneously he said, 'look up Sir 6:14-17, where you will discover God's point of view.' Incidentally, I'm quite sure that he had no idea beforehand what the passage was about. We opened the bible at the nominated text, only to find that it was about the joys of friendship. It said, 'Faithful friends are a sturdy shelter; whoever finds one finds a treasure. Faithful friends are beyond price, no amount can balance their worth. Faithful friends are life-saving medicine; those who fear God will find them. Those who fear the Lord enjoy stable friendship, for as they are, so will their neighbours be' (Sir 6:14-17). That ended all discussion. We felt that God was encouraging us to live after the manner of dear friends by cultivating unity of mind and heart.

At a memorable meeting, sometime later, one member of the community group read Lk 6:36-39 and shared how this passage, about a merciful way of life, had inspired her. When she finished, she spontaneously knelt on the floor and promised she would refrain from criticising, judging or condemning anyone in the group in thought or word. She ended by saying that if she broke her promise, in any way, she would confess the fault to the group and seek forgiveness. Her words had a remarkable effect. One by one, everyone present knelt down and made the same promise.

THE EFFECTS OF INTERPERSONAL COMMUNION
This mutual commitment had a remarkable effect.

- Firstly, we felt more closely united than ever because our trust levels had grown. We were no longer afraid of criticism when we were not personally present. Our community became a place of belonging and psychological safety where each person could afford to be his or her real self, without putting on an act in order to please others and avoid negative comments.

- Secondly, we had always been committed to praising the Lord, but when we became more united, there was more joy. A new gift of praise that was long and loud was released. One of our favourite scriptural verses was from Sir 43:31-34, 'Lift up your voices to glorify the Lord, though he is still beyond your power to praise; extol him with renewed strength, and weary not, though you cannot reach the end; for who can see him and describe him? Or who can praise him as he is?'

- Thirdly, having become more closely united, we found that there was a flowering of the spiritual gifts mentioned in 1 Cor 12:8-10.

- Fourthly, around the time that these developments were taking place we repeatedly asked God to prompt some priest to invite us to conduct an outreach together in his parish. After about two months, our prayers were answered when the parish priest of a rural area in the mountains of Tyrone invited all sixteen of us to conduct a mini-mission. The day before we headed off I was apprehensive about the impending visit. I prayed for guidance and was led to a passage in Josh 1:9, 'I hereby command you: Be strong and courageous; do not be frightened or dismayed, for the Lord your God is with you wherever you go.' When we reached the village the following day, we assembled in the sacristy of the church to pray together. I asked, if anyone had received a word of guidance for the day. One of the men answered yes, and read out Josh 1:9, the very verse I had received in prayer the day before! Then we all confidently headed off in twos to visit homes. Later we had a service of reconciliation, followed by a mass of healing. As a result, many people were reconciled to Christ and a small number were healed of physical and emotional ailments. That mini-mission stands out in my memory because it taught us about the vital link that exists between unity in the community and fruitful evangelisation.

Resolving conflicts
Inevitably conflicts will arise both within and between communities. As Pope Francis pointed out in par. 227 of *The Joy of the Gospel*, there are good and bad ways of dealing with it. 'When conflict arises,

- Some people simply look at it and go their way as if nothing happened; they wash their hands of it and get on with their lives.
- Others embrace it in such a way that they become its prisoners; they lose their bearings, project onto institutions their own confusion and dissatisfaction and thus make unity impossible.
- But there is also a third way, and it is the best way to deal with conflict. It is the willingness to face it head on, to resolve it and to make it a link in the chain of a new process. I have found that it can be helpful, with the consent of the community, to invite a trained facilitator to help the members to express any negative emotions they might be feeling. For example, the facilitator could instruct everyone to avoid 'you' statements, such as 'you are very insensitive.' and to begin instead with 'I' statements, e.g., 'I felt hurt and annoyed when you corrected me in front

of my friends yesterday.' This kind of group dynamic helps people to express what they feel, increases mutual understanding, and leads to mutual forgiveness. In this way it helps to diffuse tension.

CONCLUSION

I am absolutely convinced that unity of mind and heart is the *sine qua non* for all effective evangelisation. Every group needs to deal with the negative attitudes and feelings that are inimical to its unity. The extent to which they are unacknowledged and left unresolved is the extent to which the Holy Spirit will be quenched in the community. That being so conflict resolution and reconciliation by means of mutual, heartfelt forgiveness are vital for the family, prayer group, religious community or parish that hopes to evangelise in the power of the Holy Spirit.

SUGGESTED QUESTIONS FOR REFLECTION AND/OR DISCUSSION

- Would you agree that the members of Christian communities should relate to one another after the manner of dear friends in a warm hearted, affectionate way, or is that too much to expect?

- Could the members of your family, community, or group promise not to judge or condemn one another in thought and word, and to seek forgiveness if they failed to do so?

- Conflicts are inevitable in the Christian community. More often than not they are the result of weakness rather than malice. How can they be resolved?

THIRTEEN

ECUMENISM AND EVANGELISATION

Many of us grew up as the Counter-Reformation in the Catholic Church was coming to an end. It had held sway from the end of the Council of Trent in 1563 to the announcement of the forthcoming second Vatican Council in 1959. I can remember my mother telling me about it when I was 14. When I asked her what the Council aimed to do, she said, 'I think it is going to try to heal the rift between the Catholic and Protestant Churches.' She wasn't far wrong. In 1964 the *Decree on Ecumenism* began with these words, 'The restoration of unity among all Christians is one of the principal concerns of the Second Vatican Council... division openly contradicts the will of Christ, scandalises the world, and damages the holy cause of preaching the Gospel to every creature.' I think that the connection between inter-church unity and effective evangelisation is a vital one.

THE IMPORTANCE OF RENEWAL IN THE SPIRIT

When I was ordained a few years after the ending of the Council, I was sent to St. Patrick's College in Armagh. The troubles were at their height at the time. During that period of social turmoil I felt a growing spiritual dissatisfaction within myself. I knew something was missing in my life, but couldn't put my finger on what it was. On Feb. 4th 1974 I heard Rev Cecil Kerr, of the Church of Ireland, speaking about the fact that Jesus is our peace and how he breaks down the dividing wall between Jews and Gentiles, Catholics and Protestants. Quite frankly, his inspired words moved me to tears. I wanted to know the Lord the way he already did. I told him what I desired. He read a memorable passage from Eph 3:16-20. Then he began to pray over me, firstly in English, then in tongues. Suddenly, and effortlessly, I too began to pray fluently in tongues. I knew with great conviction that Jesus loved me, accepted me as I was and was living within me. As a result of that religious awakening, I was fully persuaded that the Lord was strongly at work in members of other churches.

Church unity and evangelisation are inseparable

Afterwards Cecil and I became great friends and ministered together in Catholic and Protestant parishes. He used to say that there would be no genuine reconciliation without renewal in the Holy Spirit, and no genuine renewal in the Holy Spirit without reconciliation. Over the years I witnessed the fact that once Catholics and Protestants were baptised in the Holy Spirit they had a God prompted desire to work for inter-church reconciliation and to carry out the great commission separately and together. You may recall that Pope John Paul II visited Ireland in 1979. When he spoke to ecumenical leaders in Dublin he confirmed what we already believed when he said, 'Only in perfect unity can we Christians adequately give witness to the truth.' Some years later John Paul reiterated that point in par.

54 of *The Church in Europe* when he said, 'Evangelisation and unity, evangelisation and ecumenism are indissolubly linked.' Over the years I have learned many things about the connection between ecumenism and evangelisation.

1. The importance of right relationships

Right relationships between Catholics and Protestants are a prerequisite for right understanding and right action. For example, if a group of Protestants and Catholics want to discuss a contentious theological issue or to make a controversial decision, e.g., opposing same sex marriage, it could only be done successfully within the context of loving fellowship. What is needed is a spirit of humility, mutual reverence and service. As St. Paul says in Phil 2:3-4, 'Do nothing out of selfish ambition or vain conceit, but in humility consider others better than yourselves. Each of you should look not only to your own interests, but also to the interests of others.' Pope Francis adds in par. 244 of *The Joy of the Gospel,* 'we must have sincere trust in our fellow pilgrims, putting aside all suspicion or mistrust, and turn our gaze to what we are all seeking: the radiant peace of God's face.' Because he believes this point is so important, the Anglican Archbishop of Canterbury, Justin Welby, has invited four members of the French *Chemin Neuf* community, a Catholic foundation with an ecumenical vocation, to live and pray at Lambeth Palace. Over the years I have found that many of those who are engaged in ecumenism become dear friends.

2. Right relationships and doctrinal understanding

Loving relationships are the interpretative key that helps

members of different churches to come to a common understanding of important Christian truths. For example in the late 1990's a memorable dialogue took place between Evangelicals and Catholics in Northern Ireland. The most contentious issue they faced was that of justification. As a result of a lot of prayer, the bonds of fellowship remained strong, and as a result, the group published an agreed statement on justification in *Evangelicals and Catholics Together in Ireland*. Soon afterwards it was superseded by par. 15 of the *Joint Declaration on Justification by the Lutheran World Federation and the Catholic Church*. That momentous statement resolved one of the most contentious and divisive issues that resulted from the Reformation.

3. Focusing on what we share in common
In par. 246 of *The Joy of the Gospel*, Pope Francis rightly says, 'If we concentrate on the convictions we share, and if we keep in mind the principle of the hierarchy of truths, we will be able to progress decidedly towards common expressions of proclamation, service and witness.' One thing we all agree upon is the core Christian message, or kerygma. As St Paul says in Eph 4:3-6, ' There is one body and one Spirit - just as you were called to one hope when you were called - one Lord, one faith, one baptism; one God and Father of all, who is over all and through all and in all.' Arguably what Paul said contains the six main points mentioned in chapter eight. It is this message that lies at the heart of a number of courses such as The Life in the Spirit Seminars, The Philip Course and the Alpha Course. Although it was devised by the Anglican Church, Alpha is being

used by all churches, including the Catholic Church, because it is kerygmatic and in accord with the Nicean Creed which we all share. Speaking about the kerygma, Pope Francis said in par. 164 of *The Joy of the Gospel*, 'The first announcement or kerygma needs to be at the centre of all evangelising activity.' I may say in passing that the joint statement on justification means that the different churches understand the kerygma in the same way.

4. The gifts of the Spirit, reconciliation & evangelisation

The gifts of the Spirit, which are sometimes exercised by Protestants and Catholics, can not only break down religious prejudices they can also manifest the coming of the Kingdom of God. For example, a Catholic woman in Northern Ireland told me that when she was shopping in a store in a Protestant area she happened to get into conversation with a fellow customer who told her that she had suffered for fifteen years from a painful physical ailment. The Catholic woman asked if she would like to be prayed with. Presuming that the woman who was going to pray for her was a Protestant, she said 'yes.' The discrete prayer lasted for only a few minutes. Then the women parted. A few days later the Protestant woman returned to the shop looking for information about the person who had in fact healed her. She described what she looked like. The shop keeper told her that she was a Catholic woman from a nearby town. The Protestant woman was amazed because up to then she thought that Catholics could not be saved. Later, the shopkeeper contacted his Catholic customer to tell her of the good news. Not surprisingly, when a Christian performs a deed of power for a member of another Church, not only does it manifest the presence and power of God's kingdom, it also tends to break down the barriers that sometimes separate Catholics from Protestants and visa versa. In other words deeds of power can be a powerful means of reconciliation and evangelisation.

5. Learning from one another

Protestants and Catholics can learn from one another in so many ways. As Pope Francis says in par. 246 of *The Joy of the Gospel*, 'How many important things unite us! If we really believe in the abundantly free working of the Holy Spirit, we can learn so much from one another!' Many years ago I heard Frenchman Fr. Daniel Ange speak about ecumenism. He said that the last thousand years were marked by growing division in the Christian Church, beginning with the 11th century split between the Catholic and Orthodox churches. That was followed by the 16th century split between the Catholic Church and the Reformed Churches. Fr Ange said that the coming era would be an age of convergence when each church would return with the spiritual and practical treasures it had discovered during its time apart. Surely, it is already happening. For example, when Archbishop Salvatore Fisichella, the head of the Pontifical Council for the New Evangelisation, was interviewed on Canadian T.V. and asked for an outstanding example of the new evangelisation in action, he cited the Alpha Course which is Anglican in origin. There is so much that Catholics and Protestants can learn from one another.

6. Proclaiming the kerygma together

When Catholics and Protestants evangelise, by proclaiming the kerygma together, there is a greater blessing. I can recall an occasion when a number of Catholics and Protestants were invited to conduct a day of renewal in Larne in Northern Ireland. David McKee, a Presbyterian minister gave the talks. Afterwards he asked a Catholic lay man, an Anglican vicar, and myself to join him in praying for people. As we did so, many of them, Catholics and Protestants alike, began to fall to the ground under the power of the Spirit. When the meeting was over, David called me aside. 'That is the first time I have ever seen people resting in the Spirit' he said, 'why do you think it has happened?' 'As far as I'm concerned,' I replied, 'There can be only one answer. God is honouring our united witness, by blessing our ministry in a special way. As Ps 133 says: 'How good and delightful it is to live together as brothers and sisters... for there Yahweh bestows a blessing.'

Conclusion

We can thank God for the wonderful ecumenical progress that has been made in the last few decades. Increasingly, Protestants and Catholics are bearing joint witness to Christ and his Gospel. Nowadays, ecumenism is including Messianic Jews who believe in Jesus as the promised Messiah, the Son of God, and their Saviour. Surely Nicky Gumbel was correct when he said at an Alpha Conference on Unity in 2015, 'Unity around Jesus is the key to the evangelisation of a nation.' We end with some words spoken by Pope Benedict XVI in December 2012, to members of the Pontifical Council for Christian Unity, 'Unity is on the one hand the fruit of faith and, on the other, a means - almost a prerequisite - for an increasingly credible proclamation of the faith to those who do not yet know the Saviour or who, while having received the proclamation of the Gospel, have almost forgotten this valuable gift.'

Suggested questions for reflection and/or discussion

- St. Augustine is thought to have said: 'in essentials, unity; in doubtful matters, liberty; in all things, charity.' Are Augustine's words relevant where ecumenism is concerned?

- Would you agree with the saying that there is no genuine renewal without reconciliation?

- Can Catholics and Protestants evangelise together?

FOURTEEN

INTERCESSION FOR EVANGELISERS

In par. 281 of *The Joy of the Gospel*, Pope Francis says, 'One form of prayer moves us particularly to take up the task of evangelisation and to seek the good of others: it is the prayer of intercession.' For instance, it would be especially appropriate in the period before a parish mission or an evangelistic outreach such as the Alpha Course.

In 2 Cor 4:4, St. Paul said that one reason why attempts to evangelise can be ineffective, is because, 'The god of this age [i.e. Satan] has blinded the minds of unbelievers so that they cannot see the light of the Gospel.' However, Paul went on to say in 2 Cor 10:3-5 that, 'For though we live in the world, we do not wage war as the world does. The weapons we fight with are not the weapons of the world.' Intercessory prayer is the number one spiritual weapon.

Those who wish to serve as partners in intercession, e.g., the housebound, the elderly, or those who are ill, could undertake to offer their sufferings for the sake of effective evangelisation and to say the following prayer every day.

Daily Prayer For Evangelisers

Father in heaven, you so loved the world that you sent your divine Son to be our redeemer. I thank you that, not only have I and countless others been baptised and confirmed into his saving death and resurrection, we also have the inner assurance that our sins, though many, are forgiven and forgotten, not through any merit of our own, but by the free gift of your Spirit.

Lord Jesus, evangelisers cannot bear effective witness to you without the energising fire of your Holy Spirit, which was first cast upon the earth on Pentecost Sunday. Help all evangelisers, by means of prayer and scripture reading, to fan into a mighty flame the gift they have already received, while expressing their gratitude for it by means of good works, especially that of bearing witness to the Gospel.

Enlighten the minds and hearts of all evangelisers to know how and when to proclaim the Good News in word and deed, even to the point of healings and miracles, so that they may astonish and amaze the profane and secular world in which we live. Preserve all evangelisers, as well as those they seek to evangelise, from the illusions and false inspirations of the evil one.

Lord, you have said in repeated messages of a prophetic kind that a great age of evangelisation is about to be inaugurated by you, one which will usher in a new Springtime for Christianity. Help all evangelisers to become effective instruments of your saving purposes. Amen.

GROUP INTERCESSION FOR EVANGELISERS

Like all Christians, the New Springtime Community is dedicated to fulfilling the great commission of Jesus and the call of the contemporary Church for a new evangelisation. The community has been led in prayer to focus on chapters two and four of the book of Nehemiah. We interpret them in symbolic terms.

Firstly, the aim of rebuilding the breached walls of Jerusalem represents God's call to contemporary Christians to restore the Church by means of evangelisation and renewal.

Secondly, the rubble lying in front of the city walls represents those worldly attachments, desires and bad habits in the lives of believers which weaken the work of evangelisation. The more such obstacles can be identified and removed the better.

Thirdly, the enemy, i.e., the evil one, exploits the rubble in order to camouflage his malevolent presence and to mount unexpected attacks, by means of circumstances and people, on those who are engaged on rebuilding the walls. St Peter warns, 'Your enemy the devil prowls around like a roaring lion looking for someone to devour' (1 Pt 5:8).

Fourthly, Nehemiah appointed half of his volunteers to keep watch for the enemy in order to warn the builders so that the evangelists and intercessors could repel the attacks together. This represents the need for spiritual discernment. As Paul says in 1 Thess 5:20-22, 'Test everything. Hold on to the good. Avoid every kind of evil.'

Fifthly, successful spiritual warfare is made possible by means of prophetic intercession in the Spirit, the sword of the word for offence and the shield of faith for defence (cf. Eph 6: 16-17). As we have already seen in 2 Cor 10:4-6 spiritual combat will be effective because it 'brings all thoughts captive to Christ.'

Mindful of these truths evangelisers are aware that their work needs to be backed up by a lot of intercessory prayer. As the Lord says in Ezech 22:30, 'I have been looking for someone among them... to man the breach in front of me, to defend the country.' We would request intercessory groups of six to eight people to commit themselves on one specified occasion each month to fast and intercede for the work of evangelisers. How the person fasts is up to him or her, e.g., skipping one or more meals in the day, or relying on unbuttered bread and water etc. Furthermore we would hope that such groups would find the following guidelines helpful.

Ten Guidelines for Intercessory Prayer

1. Appoint someone to take responsibility for leading the intercessory session by keeping the guidelines in mind, suggesting when to move from one point to another, and ending the meeting within a specified time limit. Ideally, each member of the group should have a prayer partner who intercedes for them on a regular basis between meetings.

2. Make a conscious act of faith in the presence and power of God.

3. Ask the Holy Spirit to fill you and to guide your time of intercession by means of a spirit of wisdom and revelation. Speaking about this kind of prayer Johannes Facius says in his book *God's Prophetic Agenda* (Lancaster: Sovereign World Ltd., 2009), 'We need spiritual revelation and divine light to be able to see what God sees in the whole situation. We need to come away from looking at things from a physical perspective and instead see them from a heavenly position.'

4. Spend some time in worship by thanking, praising and adoring the Lord. As Ps 144:2 assures us, 'He is my loving God and my fortress, my stronghold and my deliverer, my shield, in whom I take refuge.'

5. In Eph 6:18 we read, 'Pray in the Spirit on all occasions with all kinds of prayers and requests. With this in mind, be alert and always keep on praying for all the saints.' In Is 62:6-7 we are told that intercessory prayer should be persistent and insistent, 'I have posted watchmen on your walls, O Jerusalem; they will never be silent day or night. You who call on the Lord, give yourselves no rest.'

6. Speaking about communal intercession pars. 45-46 of the *General Instruction of the Roman Missal* say, 'In the general intercessions or prayer of the faithful, the people, exercising their priestly function, intercede for all humanity. It is appropriate that this prayer be included in all Masses celebrated with a congregation, so that petitions will be offered:

- For the Church,
- Civil authorities,
- Those oppressed by various needs,
- All young people
- The salvation of the world.

7. Pope Francis has proposed using the five finger prayer during times of intercession. Using the fingers on your hand, start with the thumb and pray these intentions in this order:

- The thumb is closest finger to you. So start praying for those who are closest to you. They are the persons easiest to remember. To pray for our dear ones is a 'Sweet Obligation.'
- The next finger is the index. Pray for those who teach you, instruct you and heal you. They need the support and wisdom to offer direction to others. Always keep them in your prayers.
- The following finger is the tallest. It reminds us of our leaders, the governors and those who have authority. They need God's guidance.
- The fourth finger is the ring finger. Even though it may surprise you, it is our weakest finger. It should remind us to pray for the weakest, the sick or those plagued by problems. They need your prayers.
- And finally we have our smallest finger, the smallest of all. Your pinkie should remind you to pray for yourself. When you are done praying for the other four groups, you will be able to see your own needs but in the proper

perspective, and also you will be able to pray for your own needs in a better way. Strictly speaking this is petitionary rather than intercessory prayer.

8. At this point blank your mind, pray in tongues for a while and ask the Spirit to guide your prayer by means of the charisms of revelation such as inspired thoughts, intuitions, a vision, word of knowledge, or scripture reading. As Gal 5:18 says 'be guided by the Spirit.' One could refer to this kind of prayer as prophetic intercession.

9. If no charismatic guidance seems to be forthcoming, intercede in an agnostic way by praying and singing in tongues, in the belief that the Spirit within is praying to God beyond. As Rom 8:26-27, 'We do not know what we ought to pray for, but the Spirit himself intercedes for us with groans that words cannot express. And he who searches our hearts knows the mind of the Spirit, because the Spirit intercedes for the saints in accordance with God's will.'

10. As the time of intercession comes to an end, thank God in the belief that the Almighty is doing immeasurably more than you can ask or think through the power of the Spirit at work within you (cf. Eph 3:20).

Suggested questions for reflection and/or discussion

- Why do you think that Pope Francis said in par.281 of *The Joy of the Gospel*, 'One form of prayer moves us particularly to take up the task of evangelisation and to seek the good of others: it is the prayer of intercession.'

- When intercessors say that they are involved in spiritual warfare, what do you think that they mean?

- Why is a spirit of wisdom and revelation important in intercessory prayer?

Section Five:

Forms and Means of Evangelisation

FIFTEEN

Person to Person Evangelisation

Although Jesus preached to crowds of people he also engaged in person-to-person evangelisation e.g. with Nicodemus (Jn 3:1-5), Zacchaeus (Lk 19:1-5), Simon the Pharisee (Lk 7:35-47) and the woman at the well (Jn 4:4-42). In the latter account Jesus accepted the Samaritan without a hint of judgment or condemnation and used the topic of water as a steppingstone to a conversation about new life in the Spirit.

In the New Testament Church the disciples usually preached to, and taught crowds, but like Jesus they also engaged in person-to-person evangelisation. There is an interesting example of this in Acts 8:26-42. It recounts how, in obedience to an inspiration of the Lord, Philip the evangelist travelled down a deserted desert road where he met an Ethiopian official. He noticed that the official was reading a manuscript. It became a stepping stone to a conversation about Jesus when Philip asked him if he understood what he was reading. The Ethiopian said that he could not do so unless someone explained it to him. That gave Philip an opportunity to talk about the Lord as the lamb of God and suffering servant, who died for the forgiveness of our sins. Soon afterwards, the court official asked to be baptised as a Christian.

The contemporary Church continues to advocate one-to-one evangelisation. Pope Paul VI said in par. 46 of *Evangelisation in the Modern World*, 'Side by side with the collective proclamation of the gospel, the other form of evangelisation, the person-to-person one, remains valid and important.' In par. 127 of *The Joy of the Gospel*, Pope Francis has written, 'There is a kind of preaching that falls to each of us as a daily responsibility... This is the informal preaching that takes place in the middle of a conversation... Being a disciple means being constantly ready to bring the love of Jesus to others, and this can happen unexpectedly and in any place: on the street, in a city square, during work, on a journey.' One-to-one evangelisation can take many forms such as a parent talking to a child about Jesus; a man sharing his faith with a friend, relative or colleague; or engaging in house to house visitation; doing street contact work; or exploiting providential opportunities to talk to strangers about meaning of life issues.

1. Identify steppingstones to faith

Pope Paul VI once said in par. 55 of *Evangelisation in the Modern World*, 'one cannot deny the existence of real steppingstones to Christianity, and of evangelical values at least in the form of a sense of emptiness or nostalgia. It would not be an exaggeration to say that there exists a powerful and tragic appeal to be evangelised.' In par. 88 of *The Joy of the Gospel* Pope Francis said, 'The Gospel tells us constantly to run the risk of a face-to-face encounter with others, with their physical presence which challenges us, with their pains and their pleas, with their joy which infects us in our close and continuous interaction.' He went on in pars 127-129 to offer advice on person-to-person evangelisation. For example he said, 'The first step is personal dialogue, when the other person speaks and shares his or her joys, hopes and concerns for loved ones, or so many other heartfelt needs. Only afterwards is it possible to bring up God's word, perhaps by reading a Bible verse or relating a story, but always keeping in mind the fundamental message: the personal love of God who became man, who gave himself up for us, who is living and who offers us his salvation and his friendship.' So, those who want to engage in person-to-person evangelisation need to look out for steppingstones to faith. Here are three examples:

- Recently a conscientious Catholic woman called Anne did a nursing exam. When it was finished, she was talking to a colleague called Liz about how things had gone. Liz said that she had been tired because she had slept badly the previous night and was also very anxious throughout the exam. Then Anne said that she had slept well and was surprisingly calm. Liz asked how she had managed it. Anne said that she had prayed to God for help and had trusted in divine help. As someone who had drifted away from the Church Liz was not only surprised she was also interested and asked Anne to tell her more about relying on God.

- Dave, a Catholic taxi driver said at a men's retreat that he tried to evangelise when he was driving around the city. He explained that often a passenger would sit beside him in the front seat. For the sake of conversation he or she might ask Dave when he had come on duty. He would respond by saying, 'I attended Mass in my local Church at 8.00 a.m. and came on duty afterwards.' Often the passenger would be curious and go on to ask questions about his beliefs. This gave Dave an opportunity of sharing the Good News about Jesus and what he has done for us.

- On their way back from Italy two Irishmen had a cup of coffee in the airport restaurant. One of them noticed that the man sitting opposite had a magazine about motorcycles. He initiated a conversation by asking if the stranger had a motorbike himself. That led to a meandering chat that went from computers to the *De Vinci Code*, to health and spirituality. The other Irishman who had been listening for quite a while, asked the American if he believed in Jesus. That question led to a dialogue about the bible, belief, and the value of doing an Alpha course. The encounter ended with a vocal prayer that the stranger would have an experience of God's love through an outpouring of the Holy Spirit.

In these three instances person-to-person evangelisation was made possible by identifying a stepping stone that could lead to a conversation about the Lord. It should also be said that a believer can also raise meaning of life issues in a more direct way. For example, if a colleague at work talks about someone who has died, you could use the opportunity to ask, 'what exactly do you think happens after death?' That question can initiate a really good conversation about faith issues.

2. Personal testimony and witness

John Paul II said something similar in par. 91 of *The Mission of the Redeemer*, 'The missionary must be... a witness to the experience of God, and must be able to say with the apostles: 'that which we have looked upon... concerning the word of life, ...we proclaim also to you' (1 Jn 1:1-3).' In 2010 Benedict XVI reiterated what his predecessors had said in his letter, *Everywhere and Always*, 'To proclaim fruitfully the Word of the Gospel one is first asked to have a profound experience of God.' So not surprisingly John Paul II once observed in par. 42 of *Mission of the Redeemer*, 'People today put more trust in... experience than in dogma.' That being so it is important to share one's personal faith story with others. It is advisable that Christians who wish to evangelise others should write down a brief account of their own conversion. Ideally it should be structured as follows.

> A. What were you like before you developed a personal relationship with Jesus Christ?
> B. How did you come to relate to Jesus in a more intimate way and to experience the free gift of his saving mercy and love?
> C. How did your new found relationship with Jesus have a transforming effect on you?

Whereas many of our contemporaries are resistant to preaching of any kind, they do respect people's personal experience, especially when it is shared in a sincere and humble way.

3. Friendship evangelisation

One of the most likely forms that person-to-person evangelisation will take is what has been referred to as friendship evangelisation, i.e., where one friend shares his or her faith story with another. If there is any factor that turns up over and over in conversion stories, it is the role played by the convert's contacts with Catholic friends. A U.S. survey of 15,000 converts was conducted on the primary influence in their conversion. It discovered that 80% was the result of friendship evangelism. It is not clear whether the statistics refer to conversion from one Church to another, or conversion to Christ.

4. House to house visitation

Much as clergy might want to visit all the families in their area, many hard pressed priests do not have the time to do so. However, parish pastoral councils can arrange for parishioners to do such visitation in twos. They could engage in a census on behalf of the parish or talk to people about parish activities and to speak, if appropriate, about faith issues. The idea is not new. The Legion of Mary have been conducting such visits for many years. It has enabled its members to contact practicing Catholics, the un-churched, and unbelievers. Many of the people who attend the Rite of Christian Initiation for adults (RCIA), with a view of becoming Catholics, have been contacted in this way.

In the Summer of 2009 there was a large mission in a number of parishes in Galway City, in the West of Ireland. A few hundred lay people volunteered to help. One thing they were trained to do was to make house to house visitations. Many of the participants said that when they began calling to people they did not know, they felt nervous and apprehensive. However, when they introduced themselves they usually got a good reception. Apart from telling people about the mission, they looked for opportunities to talk to them about faith issues. They kept in mind the six points of the kerygma, which were mentioned in chapter eight. They spoke about them if it seemed appropriate. As a general guideline they aimed to talk at some point about the person of Jesus.

Conclusion

These are just a few of the ways that we can do one-to-one evangelisation. What is needed is conviction and courage. We have to overcome our fears, and like the first disciples have a spirit of boldness. In Acts 4:30 we read that they prayed, 'Enable your servants to speak your word with great boldness.' In Eph 6:19-20 we read, 'Pray also for me, that whenever I open my mouth, words may be given me so that I will fearlessly make known the mystery of the gospel, for which I am an ambassador in chains. Pray that I may declare it fearlessly, as I should.' We will return to this topic in the final chapter.

SUGGESTED QUESTIONS FOR REFLECTION AND/OR DISCUSSION

- Do you find the prospect of engaging in person-to-person evangelisation a bit intimidating? If so why?

- In your past can you remember any stepping stone to faith which enabled you to engage in a conversation about Christian issues with someone else? What was the other person's reaction?

- If you were to give a testimony which describes how you moved from knowing about the person of Jesus to knowing him in person, what would you say?

SIXTEEN

PRAYER MINISTRY IN EVANGELISATION

There is a need for all of us to share the core teachings of Christianity with those we come in contact with, either on a one-to-one basis in the course of casual, everyday conversations, doing house to house visitation, or engaging in street evangelism where one talks to people about meaning of life issues. We can see such encounters as divine appointments which were intended by God, e.g., like the conversation of Jesus with the woman at the well of Samaria, or the meeting between Philip the evangelist and the Ethiopian official in the desert. They can become power encounters by means of prayer ministry. This can be the case as a result of offering to pray with the people we seek to evangelise. Speaking about person-to-person evangelisation, Pope Francis says in par. 128 of *The Joy of the Gospel*, 'If it seems prudent and if the circumstances are right, this fraternal and missionary encounter could end with a brief prayer related to the concerns which the person may have expressed. In this way they will have an experience of being listened to and understood; they will know that their particular situation has been placed before God, and that God's word really speaks to their lives.' This chapter will suggest how this can be done.

Praying for Others

No matter how well or badly an encounter of any kind has gone, evangelisers can bring it to a conclusion by:

- Asking the person they were talking to, whether he or she would like a prayer for any intention. Experience teaches that even those who are sceptical about Christianity will often reveal a need. It might be a relative who is sick, a friend whose marriage is in difficulty, or some personal need such as a financial problem or an impending driving test. The disclosure of such a need is significant because it is an acknowledgement of a certain poverty of spirit and an openness to the grace and power of God.
- The person who is evangelising can go on to ask, 'would you mind if I said that prayer with you right now?' The person being asked this question will usually say that it is okay.
- Then the evangeliser can say, 'do you mind if I place my fingers on your forehead or shoulder, it helps me to feel connected to you and the person you care about.' Again, they will often say that it is O.K.
- We encourage the person who is saying the prayer to use this little formula of words as a prelude to the prayer, 'God is love. God loves you. Because he loves you he wants what is best for you. His love is the answer to your deepest need and the needs of the people you care about. He is beginning to meet that need right now as I pray.'
- The prayer follows. It is better to say it in the present

rather than the future tense. For example, if the person has asked you to pray for her aunt Susan who is suffering from cancer, you could say something like this, 'Lord Susan is ailing from cancer. I thank you that you love her and desire what is best for her. Confident that this is so, I thank you that you are blessing her even now as I pray by giving the gift of peace to her body, mind and soul. I commend her to your care knowing that your Spirit, the Lord and Giver of life is upon her now and will continue to be at work within her. Amen'

Here are some spiritual points to keep in mind while praying:

A. Because of justification by grace God is at work within you

Firstly, when I am praying for a person, I reject any exaggerated feelings of unworthiness by regarding them as a temptation from Satan, the accuser, the one who opposes the purposes of God. I believe that as a result of being justified by grace through firm faith in Christ's saving work on the cross, I am qualified to be a channel of his blessing to others (cf. Col 1:12). As Paul assures us in Rm 8:1, 'there is now no condemnation for those in Christ Jesus.' They are declared not guilty and acquitted by the grace of God. So I affirm that the benevolent power and peace of God is about to flow into the person with whom I'm praying, in a mighty and effective way.

B. In the person of Christ

Secondly, when I am ministering to someone, I believe that I am acting in the person of Jesus Christ (cf. Phil 2:13). This point is made in par. 521 of the *Catechism of the Catholic Church,* 'Christ enables us to live in him all that he himself lived, and he lives it in us.' As St. Teresa of Avila stated in a memorable way, 'Christ has no body but yours, no hands, no feet on earth but yours. Yours are the eyes with which he looks with compassion on this world, yours are the feet with which he walks to do good, yours are the hands with which he blesses the world.'

C. The benevolence of God

Thirdly, I affirm the fact that the Lord is benevolent. In other words he wants what is best for the person I'm praying for. Jesus referred to the benevolence of God, when he said to parents, 'If you, then, though you are evil, know how to give good gifts to your children, how much more will your Father in heaven give good gifts to those who ask him!' (Mt 7:11). I heard a moving story on radio which illustrated this point. A man described, how as a boy in Derry, he had been hit on the bridge of his nose by a rubber bullet. It blinded him in both eyes. When he was brought to Altnagelvin area hospital, he heard his father ask a doctor, 'Can you save my son's eyes?' to which he replied, 'I'm afraid we cannot, the damage is too great.' Then the boy heard his father say, 'could you not take my eyes and give them to my son?' to which the doctor responded, 'Unfortunately, that will not be possible either.' St. Paul echoed that point when he said, 'He who did not spare his own Son but gave him up for us all, will he not also give us all things with him?' (Rm 8:32). If that imperfect father in Northern Ireland, wanted what was best for his son, surely our perfect Father in heaven wants what is best for his adopted sons and daughters.

D. In the power of the Spirit
Fourthly, I affirm the fact that the Holy Spirit is active in and through me. I focus on the truth that it is the same Spirit that raised Jesus from the powerlessness of death to triumphant, and glorious new life. St. Paul speaks eloquently about this in Eph 1:17-20, 'I keep asking that the God of our Lord Jesus Christ, the glorious Father, may give you the Spirit of wisdom and revelation, so that you may know... his incomparably great power for us who believe. That power is like the working of his mighty strength, which he exerted in Christ when he raised him from the dead and seated him at his right hand in the heavenly realms.' The Holy Spirit is the Lord and giver of life. Knowing this to be true, St Paul could say in Phil 4:13, 'I can do everything through him who gives me strength.' I believe that, not only is that power within me and all believers, it flows out through my hands in an authoritative way during times of ministry.

E. Praying within the will of God
Fifthly, I strive to pray for the person in accordance with the will of God and the measure of faith I have received (cf. Rm 12:3). Sometimes that is made easy because either before or during the time of ministry the Lord can give the praying person a word of revelation. It not only reveals God's specific will, but it also evokes expectant faith, because as Paul told us in Rm 10:17, 'faith comes from hearing the message, and the message is heard through the word of Christ.' Although that verse refers primarily to the kerygma, it is also true of any inspired word of God. One thing that really helps me when I'm praying for people in evangelisation situations is the belief that even if I do not know

what God's specific will is for the person, I'm utterly convinced that God wants the person to experience his peace in some way or other, i.e., blessing, wholeness, harmony, and healing of either body, mind or spirit. It is significant that when the risen Jesus appeared to the disciples, he repeatedly said to them, 'peace be with you.' So, more often than not, I pray for God's peace in the firm belief that God is granting it, in one way or another.

TESTIMONY

Some time ago I visited Southport in the North of England. I was asked to celebrate the Eucharist in a country church. When I got there I found that it was full. The gospel of the day began with the words, 'the crowd was pressing in on him to hear the word of God' (Lk 5:1). It struck me deeply and I decided to preach on that verse. I stressed the importance of having a heartfelt desire to have a personal relationship with Jesus while pointing out that such a desire is prompted within by the power of the Holy Spirit. As Jesus explained, 'No one can come to me unless the Father who sent me draws him' (Jn 6:44). When I completed the homily, we had the prayers of the faithful. Instead of offering a prayer, a man in the middle of the congregation said in a very poignant way, 'I have been pressing in to Jesus all my life and haven't got any closer.' Later in the Mass when the time for Holy Communion arrived, this man came forward to receive. When he had done so, he crossed his arms over his chest as a sign that he wanted a blessing. When I looked at him, I remembered what he had said about pressing in to know Jesus. I put my hand on his head and said in the words of St. Paul, 'I pray that out of his glorious riches he may strengthen you with power through his

Spirit in your inner being, so that Christ may dwell in your heart through faith. And I pray that you, being rooted and established in love, may have power, together with all the saints, to grasp how wide and long and high and deep is the love of Christ, and to know this love that surpasses knowledge - that you may be filled to the measure of all the fullness of God' (Eph 3:16-19).

The next day I was talking to a woman who said, 'do you remember the man who said yesterday that he could not get close to Jesus?' 'Yes' I replied. 'Well he has been crying on and off ever since.' At first I thought that perhaps his tears were those of frustration and disappointment. But before I could say anything, the woman explained that ever since receiving Holy Communion the man had experienced such a strong sense of Jesus and his love, that it had brought tears of joy to his eyes.' Later in the day I met the man himself who confirmed what the woman had told me. Clearly, he had crossed the threshold of faith. Instead of knowing about the person of Jesus as heretofore, he had come to know Jesus and his love, in person.

Conclusion

I am convinced that ministry in the power of the Spirit is a powerful and effective way of evangelising. There was a saying which was attributed to Hanina Ben Dosa, a contemporary of Jesus, 'he whose actions exceed his wisdom, his wisdom shall endure, but he whose wisdom exceeds his actions, his wisdom shall not endure.' Not surprisingly, the apostles said similar things. For instance, St. Paul testified, 'My message and my preaching were not with wise and persuasive words, but with a demonstration of the Spirit's power' (1 Cor 2:41). It is no different nowadays.

Suggested questions for reflection and/or discussion

- While you may have often promised to pray for people, have you ever offered to pray with them?

- It was suggested that to pray effectively, five points could be kept in mind. Which of them strikes you as being the most important?

- What is meant by the phrase, praying with expectant faith?

SEVENTEEN

EVANGELISATION AND DELIVERANCE FROM EVIL SPIRITS

In Gen 3;1-19; we are told that the curse and penalty of sin came into the world as a result of Adam and Eve consenting to the temptation of the devil who appeared to them in the form of a serpent. In Wis 2:23-24 we are told that, 'God formed us to be imperishable. In the image of his own nature he made us. But by the envy of the devil, death entered the world, and they who are allied with him experience it.' The death referred to in this verse refers to spiritual death (the curse of sin) and physical death (the penalty of sin). When Jesus came to bring salvation, not only did he lift the curse of sin and remove its penalty, he overcame the power of the evil one who was the origin of both.

As soon as Jesus, the new Adam, was baptised in the Jordan and filled with the Spirit he experienced three diabolical temptations which he resisted by quoting the word of God, 'the sword of the Spirit' (Eph 6:17). During his public ministry Jesus not only proclaimed the Good News, he demonstrated it by driving out evil spirits. In Mk 1:19 we read, 'He went all through Galilee, preaching in their synagogues and driving out devils.' As Jesus testified, 'If it is by the finger of God that I cast out demons, then the kingdom of God has come upon you'

(Lk 11:20). The confrontation between the devil and Jesus came to its high point in Holy Week. The devil entered the heart of Judas to betray Jesus. As the Lord hung on the cross, darkness enveloped him. It was symbolic of the presence of the prince of darkness. But when Jesus died, obedient even to death, the power of Satan was broken. As Col 2:15 assures us, 'having disarmed the powers and authorities, he made a public spectacle of them, triumphing over them by the cross.' Before he ascended into heaven, Jesus not only commissioned the apostles and disciples to proclaim the Good News, he gave them the power to demonstrate it by delivering people from evil spirits. He said to them: 'These signs will accompany those who believe, in my name they will drive out demons' (Mk 16:17). So it is clear from scripture that deliverance from evil spirits is an integral aspect of evangelisation.

Church Teaching

Does the Church still teach that the devil exists? The answer is yes. Bl. Paul VI said in a papal address: 'The question of the devil and the influence he can have on individual persons as well as communities, whole societies or events is a very important chapter of Catholic doctrine... It is a departure from the picture provided by biblical and Church teaching to refer to the devil's existence... as a pseudo reality, a conceptual and fanciful personification of the unknown causes of our misfortunes.' At the launch of the revised rite of exorcism in late 1999, Cardinal Estevez, of the Congregation of Divine Worship, reiterated the Church's teaching, 'the existence of the devil is not an opinion... It belongs to Catholic faith and doctrine... but the strategy of the devil is to convince people that he does not exist.' The cardinal then went on to suggest that the devil's malign activity helps to explain particular atrocities, such as World War II and the Holocaust. He also stated in a more general way that the devil, 'manages to trap many people - he fools them by leading them to believe that happiness can be found in money, power and sexual lust. He deceives men and women by persuading them that they do not need God and that they are self-sufficient.'

OPPRESSION AND POSSESSION

Besides suffering from psychological and physical problems, some of the people we seek to evangelise will be suffering from spiritual oppression and even possession by evil spirits. When people are oppressed, they suffer from a kind of spiritual neurosis where only part of their personality is subject to demonic influence. For instance, the devil can fill their minds with compulsive thoughts and evil inclinations, such as immoral sexual or suicidal impulses. When people are possessed, and I have to say it is a very rare occurrence, they suffer from a form of spiritual psychosis because the devil seems to take over their entire personalities. Oppression can be dealt with by means of prayer for deliverance. It can be offered by any believing Christian. Possession can be dealt with by means of the rite of exorcism which can only be conducted by a wise and mature priest appointed for that purpose by the bishop of the diocese.

How people become oppressed and possessed

Unfortunately, in contemporary society many people have separated from the living God as a result of a number of things. Here are a few examples:

- Nowadays large numbers of people revere the golden calf of possessions, popularity, and power. They tend to rewrite the commandments of God to suit themselves and, as a result, engage in activities that are seriously sinful in God's eyes. Not surprisingly, that can leave them open to the influence of evil spirits who prowl around like a roaring lion looking for someone to devour (cf. 1 Pt 5:8-9).
- There are other people who may have been severely traumatised in the past as a result of some kind of abuse or disturbing event such as being cursed by someone or discovering the body of a close relative who had hung him or herself. The devil can exploit those unhealed memories.
- Others have recourse to such things as occult, Gnostic and superstitious beliefs and practices, e.g. astrology, palmistry, spiritualism, contacting the dead, consulting mediums, and using a Ouija board or tarot cards in a misguided effort to contact the world of spirits or to gain control over their lives and their futures. In engaging in these and similar activities, people can unwittingly open themselves to the influence of evil spirits.

The need for discernment

When people ask us for prayer, we need to request God to give us a spirit of discernment, so as to be able to distinguish between what are psychological problems as opposed to spiritual oppression or possession. Some of those who ask for prayer will tell us that they are afflicted by evil spirits. However, that isn't necessarily true. The vast majority of the bizarre behaviours which were once attributed to the devil can now be explained in medical and psychiatric ways; such as schizophrenia or Tourette's syndrome which is a neurological disorder, characterised by tics, involuntary vocalisation, and often by the compulsive utterance of obscenities.

PRAYING FOR DELIVERANCE AND THE FIVE KEYS

Some of the points made in the previous chapter are relevant here. If a person really does need deliverance prayer, it is better to have two or three men and women pray for the person, with one of them taking the lead. There is reason to feel confident. Paul assures us in 2 Cor 10:3-5, 'though we live in the world, we do not wage war as the world does. The weapons we fight with are not the weapons of the world. On the contrary, they have divine power to demolish strongholds. We demolish arguments and every pretension that sets itself up against the knowledge of God, and we take captive every thought to make it obedient to Christ.' In His very helpful book *Unbound: A Practical Guide to Deliverance* (Grand Rapids: Chosen Books, 2003) Neal Lozano recommends that those engaged in deliverance prayer should use the following five keys.

Key 1. *Repentance and faith.* There is no greater deliverance than embracing the grace of baptism, by turning from sin and turning to the Lord. Jesus is our deliverer. The first key also involves ongoing repentance and conversion as the hidden sins of the heart are revealed.

Key 2. *Forgiveness.* If we want to be like Jesus we need to forgive from the heart. Many believers who know they need to forgive have failed to understand how to access the power of forgiveness that Jesus has given them. As forgiveness is pronounced by faith, and the power behind un-forgiveness is renounced, it is defeated.

Key 3. *Renunciation.* Each Easter Catholics renew their baptismal vows beginning with, 'I renounce Satan and all of his works and all of his empty promises.' Renunciation is a declaration before the kingdom of darkness that I no longer make a home for sin, deception and the power behind it. I am no longer in agreement with this lie that has been buried in my heart and my thoughts. Specifically renouncing our enemies brings victory. For example, one might state, 'I renounce fear in the name of Jesus, I renounce a spirit of rejection in the name of Jesus, I renounce lust... loneliness... a spirit of anger... resentment and bitterness... hatred. I renounce the lie that everything is my fault... I renounce the idol of fame and recognition...'

Key 4. *Authority.* When the Lord said to Moses, 'I will be an enemy to your enemies' (Ex 23:22), he did not mean that Moses would sit and watch. He meant that as Moses fought, so would God. Moses had God's authority. In Christ, we too have authority over our enemies who seek to destroy us. We can take our stand against them through repentance, forgiveness, renunciation and then declare the truth of their defeat by saying, 'In the name of Jesus I command any (or every) spirit that I have renounced to leave me now.'

Key 5. *The Father's Blessing.* The Hebrew sense of blessing means to speak words that empower someone to prosper and thrive. They are words that give life and peace. Words carry spiritual power. Every blessing that the Father spoke to Jesus is ours. The Father reveals to us who we are as we come before him in the Son. What we have longed to hear all of our lives has already been spoken. As we learn to receive His blessing, so we are healed. To be 'unbound' means that the obstacles to the gift that has been waiting for us have been removed and the Father's love and affirmation is made real to us in Christ.

Sometimes when saying prayers for deliverance the evil spirit will be manifested, e.g., you may hear the devil speak by using the person's voice. It usually sounds rougher and lower in tone than the person's customary way of speaking. Lozano is correct, I think, when he says that ministers of deliverance should focus on God and the person being prayed with rather than the devil. In my experience I have found that in many instances there may be a need for repeated prayers for deliverance before the afflicted person is completely freed from demonic influence. It is important that those being prayed with trust in Jesus and that they are conscientious in avoiding sin by devoting themselves to regular prayer and reception of the sacraments.

Conclusion

Although deliverance prayer is an important aspect of evangelisation, it is a complex and difficult one. Ideally, those who engage in it would need to be trained in the do's and dont's involved, e.g., *Unbound*. Neal Lozano has a good website entitled, Heart of the Father Ministries where free resource material is available. If a particular case proves to be too difficult to tackle it would be better, if possible, to refer the person to someone more experienced in the diocese. There are a number of helpful books available on the subject such as Francis McNutt's *Deliverance from Evil Spirits: A Practical Manual* (Grand Rapids: Chosen Books, 2009) and Peter J. Horrobin's *Healing Through Deliverance: The Foundations and Practice of Deliverance Ministry* (Lancaster: Sovereign World, 2008).

Suggested questions for reflection and/or discussion

- As Peter said in Acts 10:38, Jesus, 'went around doing good and healing all who were under the power of the devil.' Why do you think that exorcism played such an important role in the ministry of Jesus?

- How would you know whether a person needed deliverance ministry or not?

- Do you find that Lozano's five keys are helpful?

EIGHTEEN

FAMILIES AND EVANGELISATION

There is an obvious crisis of the family in modern secular culture. This is evident in the growing numbers of couples who live together without getting married, the high incidence of divorce, same sex marriage and the like. Also there is a growing rift between the sexual mores of secular society and those advocated by the church, e.g., recourse to abortion as a form of birth control. No wonder Pope Francis said in par. 66 of *The Joy of the Gospel*, 'The family is experiencing a profound cultural crisis, as are all communities and social bonds. In the case of the family, the weakening of these bonds is particularly serious because the family is the fundamental cell of society.' Not surprisingly, therefore, the Church wants to nurture Christian families as the domestic church, the focal point of the new evangelisation. It believes that evangelisation must take place both within and without the family, by means of non-verbal and verbal witness.

EVANGELISATION WITHIN THE FAMILY

Couples evangelise within marriage primarily by means of their relationship. True to the teaching of the Old and New Testaments, the Church puts forward a high ideal for marriage and family life. It believes that couples discover their innermost selves, including their God-selves, by means of self-forgetful love for one another. In the words of a well known Abba song, it is a matter of 'knowing me knowing you.' So if people want to discover *who* they are as individuals and as Christians, they need to know *whose* they are in and through their relationships. Pope John Paul made this point repeatedly in his writings.

A. Witness

The Pontiff explained how couples encounter God within themselves through their love for one another. In a profound passage in *Man and Woman He Created Them: A Theology of the Body* (Boston: Pauline, 2006), he wrote, 'The body, in fact, and only the body, is capable of making visible what is invisible, namely the spiritual and the divine. It has been created to transfer into the visible reality of the world the mystery hidden from eternity in God, and thus to be a sign of it.' Clearly John Paul believed that loving communion between spouses mediates a sense of God's presence. As the poet Hopkins put it, 'for Christ plays in ten thousand places, lovely in limbs, and lovely in eyes not his, to the Father through the features of men's faces.' The communion existing between man and wife is not only a sign of the communion that exists in the Trinity but also a graced participation in that communion. Par. 2205 of the *Catechism of the Catholic Church* echoes that point of view when it says that, 'The Christian family is a communion of persons, a sign and image of the communion of the Father and the Son in the Holy Spirit. In the procreation and education of children it reflects the Father's work of creation.'

It is in this environment of love that children experience the

Good News of God's love in and through the love of their parents. As par. 11 of the *Decree on the Apostolate of the Laity* states, 'Christian husbands and wives are co-operators in grace, and witnesses in faith for each other, their children, and all others in their household.' That being so, it could be said that in the early years of children's lives the faith is caught not taught.

B. Catechesis

While silent witness is vital, nevertheless, parents also need to pass on the faith to their children by teaching them about various aspects of the Christian religion, such as belief in Jesus, the sacraments, prayer, and kindness to others etc. In this context it is important that parents not only teach their children about prayer but also that they pray with them. In par 288 of his Apostolic Exhortation on the family, entitled, *The Joy of Love*, Pope Francis wrote, 'It is essential that children actually see that, for their parents, prayer is something truly important. Hence moments of family prayer and acts of devotion can be more powerful for evangelisation than any catechism class or sermon.' Pope Francis has many other interesting things to say about the family and evangelisation in pars. 287-290 of the same Exhortation. Sad to say, only a very small minority of Catholic families pray together. In some cases it is due to a lack of conviction and in others due to the fact that people are so busy that families rarely spend time together.

Pope John Paul II also said in par. 53 of *On the Christian Family in the Modern World*, 'The ministry of evangelisation which is carried out by Christian parents is original and irreplaceable.'

In par. 52 Pope John Paul added that, 'In places where anti-religious legislation endeavors even to prevent education in the faith, and in places where widespread unbelief or invasive secularism makes real religious growth practically impossible, 'the church of the home' remains the one place where children and young people can receive an authentic catechesis.' In our fast changing world, it is the responsibility of parents to have an informed faith. To this end they need to read, e.g., a simplified version of the *Catechism of the Catholic Church*, or to attend a Catholic adult education course, if one is available, or to seek out useful and relevant material available on the internet. Fearing the ill effects of education in secular schools, an increasing number of Catholic parents are making heroic efforts to provide their children with home schooling within a faith filled ethos. While parents teach their children, the children teach their parents, e.g., what they learnt in school. Pope Paul VI said in par. 71 of *Evangelisation in the Modern World*, 'Parents not only communicate the Gospel to their children, but from their children they can themselves receive the same Gospel as deeply lived by them.' As has already been mentioned in earlier chapters, evangelisation in the home, like all evangelisation, should be radically Christ centered.

In adult life it is not at all uncommon for one or more members of a family to drift away from Christ and the church. That situation presents an opportunity for evangelisation by another member/s of the family. As Pope John Paul II said in par. 54 of *On the Christian Family in the Modern World*, 'When some member of the family does not have the faith or does not practice it with consistency other members must give him or her a living witness of their own faith in order to encourage and support him or her along the path toward full acceptance of Christ the saviour.' In par. 288 of *The Joy of Love*, Pope Francis said, 'I would like to express my particular gratitude to all those mothers who continue to pray, like Saint Monica, for their children who have strayed from Christ.' It has to be admitted, however, that for many reasons it is not easy to evangelise another family member.

GRANDPARENTS

Grandparents also have an important role to play, especially in cases where a son or daughter no longer goes to church. Speaking about this point in Brazil, Pope Francis stated, 'I would like to say... how important grandparents are for family life, for passing on the human and religious heritage which is so essential for each and every society! How important it is to have intergenerational exchanges and dialogue, especially within the context of the family.' Catherine Wiley, a glamorous Irish grandmother, was so convinced of the importance of this point that she founded the Catholic Grandparents Association. It points out that:

- Grandparents can pray for their grandchildren.
- Grandparents can teach their grandchildren prayers they do not know. Sad to say, often non-practicing parents fail to do this, or to bring their children to church, or to send them to Catholic schools.
- Grandparents can give their grand-children, age

appropriate versions of the Bible, and talk to them about Bible stories.
- Grandparents can bring their grandchildren to Church events, especially the Eucharist.
- Grandparents can act as witnesses to divine mercy and kindness by their own non- judgmental, and non-condemnatory attitudes.
- Grandparents can talk about what God, Jesus, Mary and the saints mean to them.
- Some grandparents secretly baptise their un-baptised grandchildren without their parent's consent. Though well intentioned the Church says they should not do this. Par. 868 of *The Code of Canon Law* states, 'For an infant to be baptised lawfully, it is required that the parents, or at least one of them, or the person who lawfully holds their place, give their consent.'

EVANGELISATION BY THE FAMILY

As a domestic church and the primary cell of society, the Christian family is called by God to engage in evangelisation. It does so by means of the witness of its way of life and by talking about the values and beliefs that inform its loving communion. Pope Francis talks about this subject in 'Passing on the Faith' in pars. 287-290 of his Apostolic Exhortation, *Love and Joy*.

A. *Witness*

All of us have come across outstanding Christian families. That said, they all have weaknesses and problems. That is par for the course. But what really impresses the people who know such families is the way in which they respond to human frailty with compassion and love. For example, a teenage daughter gets pregnant. Instead of berating her, she experiences acceptance and love from her parents; instead of encouraging her to get an abortion they assure her that they will give her every help she needs in order to raise her child.

In par. 11 of *The Decree on the Apostolate of the Laity*, the fathers of the Second Vatican Council wrote, 'Among the various activities of the family apostolate the following may be enumerated: the adoption of abandoned infants, hospitality to strangers, assistance in the operation of schools, helpful advice and material assistance for adolescents, help to engaged couples in preparing themselves better for marriage, catechetical work, support of married couples and families involved in material and moral crises, help for the aged not only by providing them with the necessities of life but also by obtaining for them a fair share of the benefits of an expanding economy.' There are outstanding families that do many of these things. For example, there is an admirable Catholic family that runs a retreat centre called Craig Lodge in Dalmally, Scotland. One of the family members, Magnus MacFarlane-Barrow is the founder of a charity called Mary's Meals which provides a meal to 920,000 poor children daily. What a witness.

B. *Verbal Evangelisation*
Loving Christian families are hospitable. They welcome both friends and strangers into their homes. When visitors experience the sense of belonging, love and joy that the family enjoys, it

often prompts them to ask questions which can lead to evangelising opportunities as the family members talk about the beliefs and values that inform their lives together. As we read in 1 Pt 3:15, 'Always be prepared to give an answer to everyone who asks you to give the reason for the hope that you have. But do this with gentleness and respect.' Verbal evangelisation by family members will include many of the methods described in previous chapters such as the ones which deal with person-to-person evangelisation and praying with those we seek to evengelise.

Conclusion

We end with some words spoken by Pope Benedict XVI to a plenary assembly of the Pontifical Council for the Family. He began by saying that the New Evangelisation is 'inseparable' from Catholic family life. Then he went on to add, 'in our time, as in the past, the eclipse of God, the spread of an anti-family ideology and the abasement of sexual morality appear interconnected.' This is why 'the New Evangelisation is inseparable from the Christian family. The family is the Church's 'path,' because it is a 'human place' in which we encounter Christ, 'like the Church, the family is called to live, radiate and express to the world the love and presence of Christ.'

Suggested questions for reflection and/or discussion

- How can parents evangelise their children while respecting their freedom?

- How can grandparents best pass on the faith to their grandchildren?

- How can the members of a family evangelise people outside their home?

NINETEEN

EVANGELISATION OF AND BY YOUNG ADULTS

Young adulthood refers to people in their late teens, twenties, and thirties; single, married, divorced, or widowed; and with or without children. They are present in every trade and profession. They live in the many communities that make up our society - from rural areas to small towns to large cities. They come from diverse cultural, ethnic, educational, vocational, social, political, and spiritual backgrounds. Typically young adults were raised with music, television, and the rapid explosion of information technology. They are a generation that some social scientists call the first truly multicultural and multimedia generation.

IGNORANCE OF CHRISTIAN TEACHING

When Pope John Paul II spoke to the young adults at Galway in 1979 he warned, 'The religious and moral traditions of Ireland, the very soul of Ireland, will be challenged by temptations that spare no society in our age. Like so many other young people in various parts of the world, you will be told that changes must be made, that you must have more freedom, that you should be different from your parents, and that the decisions about your lives depend on you, and you alone,' in *The Pope in Ireland: Addresses and Homilies* (Dublin: Veritas, 1979). Then he went on to highlight certain dangers:

- The prospect of growing economic progress, and the chance of obtaining a greater share of the goods that modern society has to offer, will appear to you as an opportunity to achieve greater freedom.
- The lure of pleasure, to be had whenever and wherever it can be found, will be strong and it may be presented to you as part of progress towards greater autonomy and freedom from rules. How many young people have already warped their consciences and have substituted the true joy of life with drugs, sex, alcohol, vandalism and the empty pursuit of mere material possessions.
- You will hear people tell you that your religious practices are hopelessly out of date, that they hamper your style and your future, that with everything that social and scientific progress has to offer, you will be able to organise your own lives, and that God's role is redundant.

Wouldn't it be true to say that, like many young adults in other countries, many of those in Ireland and Britain have already succumbed to those dangers.

Although the practice of religion has fallen by more than 66% in Ireland since the visit of John Paul II, the decline has been more pronounced among adolescents and young adults. Apparently only one in five of young adults go weekly to Mass. Archbishop Dermot Martin of Dublin said in a talk he gave in Cambridge, England in 2012 that, 'Young Irish people are among the most catechised in Europe but apparently among the least evangelised.' I wonder if he was overly optimistic when he talked about their catechetical instruction. An all Ireland survey conducted by Lansdowne Marketing in 2007, for the Iona Institute, discovered that most 15-24 year olds are almost entirely ignorant of basic Christian teachings.

- Only 5% could quote the first of the Ten Commandments.
- Almost one-third could not say where Jesus was born.
- More than one-third did not know what is celebrated at Easter.
- The survey found that only 52% of young people could name Matthew, Mark, Luke and John as the authors of the gospels.
- Only 38% knew that there were four gospels.
- Fewer than half of the 15 to 24 year-olds surveyed could name 'Father, Son and Holy Spirit' as the three persons of the Trinity.
- Only 48% were able to name Genesis as the first book of the Bible.
- Thirty-eight per cent were aware that there were seven Sacraments, but just 15% knew that 'transubstantiation' was the term used to describe what takes place at Mass.

In view of these facts it is not too surprising that many young adults do not attend church on a regular basis. They too are victims of the faith crisis of head, heart and hands, mentioned in chapter one. What these facts indicate is that, not only is there a need for kerygmatic type evangelisation which focuses on the person of Jesus, there is also a need for a good deal of catechesis.

The subject of evangelisation of young adults is a very large one. I will only make three observations here which are based on my own experience.

THE CALL TO COMMUNITY

In the past evangelisers tended to stress the primacy of orthodox belief and right behaviour. They were seen as necessary preconditions for a sense of belonging. In secular, postmodern society, where individualism is rampant and social alienation is common, young adults have an overriding need for a feeling of unconditional belonging. Arguably this is the essence of effective pre-evangelisation. Religious people are, literally, those who are bound together by a common experience of a love that simultaneously connects them to one another, to their deepest identities and ultimately to God. If young adults have a sense of belonging within a caring Christian community, they will be more likely to discover who they are and what they want. They will also be more open to accept the Christian beliefs that inform that community. There is a saying which is relevant in this connection, 'I sought my soul, but my soul I could not see. I sought my God, but my God eluded me. I sought my brother and I found all three.' In other words, human relationships, especially of a loving and intimate kind, can mediate the presence and the merciful love of God, who was revealed in Christ's saving life, death and resurrection. It is only within this loving context that the issue of right behaviour can be tackled. Ideally, right action should be an expression of a sense of Christian belonging and belief, rather than a dutiful requirement, as it has often seemed to be in the past. There are some parishes and groups that not only appreciate this point, they provide a no-strings-attached type fellowship to young adults who are seeking for a sense of belonging and unconditional meaning in their lives. It has been said that people have many reasons for joining the Christian community, but there is only one reason why they remain, a sense of belonging.

THE CALL TO SERVICE

Some evangelisers have discovered the value of *praxis,* especially where young adults are concerned. Instead of beginning with issues of faith, Christian mentors can encourage young adults to engage in practical action such as volunteering to serve people who are less well off in the developing world, or to participate in the kind of work that members of the St. Vincent de Paul Society do in every parish in the country. Through their contact with the poor, the elderly, the handicapped and the marginalised, the eyes and hearts of young adults are opened to the suffering of others and to the unjust structures of society that often oppress and discriminate unfairly against them. These realisations are food for reflection on values and meaning-of-life issues, in a way that often leads young men and women to ask religious type questions. Adult facilitators can assist them to engage in theological reflection on their experience. As a result, young adults who may have been alienated from Jesus and the Church may come into a new faith relationship with both.

THE CALL TO SAVING FAITH

The faith crisis of head, heart and hands, already referred to in chapter one, can only be ended as a result of kerygmatic evangelisation when the core truths of Christianity, all of which centre on the person of Jesus, are proclaimed. There are many ways of engaging in such evangelisation. Alpha has tried and tested courses which have proved to be very effective.

Firstly, there is *Explore the Christian Faith: A Programme of Study for Students Aged 11-14*. It deals with the same topics as the adult Alpha course but in a way that is adapted to the needs of young people. Although the talks are given by live speakers, there is a backup DVD which contains images, music, short films, and vox pops on subjects mentioned in the lesson outlines.

Secondly, there is *Schools Alpha: Taking Youth Alpha into Schools*. The course has been divided into three streams. Like *Exploring the Faith*, this course is taught live rather than watched on DVD. There is a back-up DVD, however, which contains all kinds of video clips, and vox-pops. This course is also backed up by Alpha for Youth, a very colourful manual in magazine form. As is usual with Alpha materials, the production values of both are very high.

Thirdly, another course has been developed for use in third level colleges and universities. *Alpha for Students* is not all that different from the typical adult one. Each week, the talk which is given by a live speaker who looks at a specific aspect of the Christian faith and is followed by discussion in the small groups. The emphasis is upon exploration and discovery in a relaxed and informal environment. This Alpha course usually lasts for 10 weeks, with a day or weekend away in the middle. Some courses are held over morning coffee or during a lunch break. However, most are evening courses which sometimes begin with pizza and a pint. Typically they last two hours and are held either in halls of residence, a student's flat, or some other venue. As with the other courses, *Alpha for Students* is backed up by excellent printed materials and a DVD.

The National Committee of Diocesan Youth Directors and the Commission for Pastoral Renewal and Adult Faith Development of the Irish Catholic Bishops' Conference has published a helpful booklet entitled, *Called Together: Making the Difference*. It aims to promote four goals.

1. To help young adults to grow, both in a personal sense and a spiritual sense.
2. To give young people the opportunity to experience what it is like to be a disciple of Jesus Christ.
3. To inspire and facilitate young adults to take an active role in the Catholic community.
4. To encourage the Catholic community to continually put aside any prejudices about young adults and to recognise and empower their talents and energy.

In Ireland there are also a number of groups that focus on the evangelisation of young adults such as Youth 2000, Catholic Youth Care, Pure in Heart, National Evangelisation Teams, and Jesus Youth, which is mainly working in the Indian community in Ireland. They all find that the book YOUCAT: *The Youth Catechism of the Catholic Church* is an effective instrument in the evangelisation of young adults. In Britain, CaFE - Catholic Faith Exploration has produced many excellent teaching materials which could be used by young adult groups for catechetical purposes.

EVANGELISATION BY YOUNG ADULTS

Having being fully evangelised themselves, young adults have a God given vocation to evangelise others, especially their peers. Happily there are young adult groups who are doing just that. It is a matter of like evangelising like. One notable example is what is known as Night Fever. It is a street evangelisation outreach which began at World Youth Day in Cologne, Germany in 2008. It involves opening a city church for the evening. Typically, young adults wearing high visibility vests, spend hours inviting people inside a church where priests are available for confession. Passers-by, many of them non church goers, come inside to light a candle in an atmosphere of music and Eucharistic Adoration. There are facilities for writing prayer requests. There is also a basket containing scripture texts. Each visitor to the church can take a text in the belief that it is the providential word of God for them. By evangelising in this way, young adults strengthen and deepen their own faith while helping to bring others to faith in Christ.

Suggested Questions for Reflection and/or Discussion

- Why are so many young Catholics ignorant of the basic teachings of their faith?

- Would you agree that although practicing Catholics lament the fact that so many young adults are un-churched, surprisingly little effort or resources, e.g., trained youth ministers, are provided in order to reach out and evangelise university students and young adult workers? Why do you think this is so?

- Why is a sense of unconditional belonging a key to the evangelisation of young adults?

TWENTY

EVANGELISING UNBELIEVERS

Every now and then when I'm reading the Bible a verse will influence me to an unusual degree. That happened some time ago when I read in Eph 2:12 that unbelievers were, 'without hope and without God in the world.' I think that Paul was speaking in objective terms. In other words, no matter what unbelievers might believe, they are in fact alienated from the true God. In par. 27 of his encyclical *The Hope of Salvation*, Pope Benedict XVI wrote, 'anyone who does not know God, even though he may entertain all kinds of hopes, is ultimately without hope, without the great hope that sustains the whole of life. Man's great, true hope which holds firm in spite of all disappointments can only be God - God who has loved us and who continues to love us.' Paul spoke again about some unbelievers in Eph 4:18-20 when he said, 'They are darkened in their understanding, alienated from the life of God because of their ignorance and hardness of heart. They have lost all sensitivity and have abandoned themselves to licentiousness, greedy to practice every kind of impurity.'

Recently I came across a poignant quote from well known film maker Woody Allen in which he said. 'I am realistic, there is no God. There is no purpose to the universe. One day the sun will burn out. Earth will be gone and further down the line the entire universe will be gone. Everything we've created will have gone: Beethoven, Shakespeare. It's a meaningless thing. I am realistic in my appraisal of the human condition.' It sounds as if Allen, like so many of his contemporaries, is without God or hope.

THE CHURCH ON ATHEISM/AGNOSTICISM
In par. 19 of the Vat II document, *The Church in the Modern World* we read, 'Atheism must be accounted among the most serious problems of this age... The word atheism is applied to phenomena which are quite distinct... while God is expressly denied by some (i.e., atheism), others believe that man can assert absolutely nothing about him (i.e., agnosticism).' Recent Popes have commented on the contemporary phenomenon of unbelief. St. John Paul II said repeatedly in his writings that pars 22 and 24 of the Vat II document on *The Church in the Modern World* were of major significance. They taught that alienation from God inevitably means alienation from one's own deeper self. For instance in par. 38 of his encyclical, *Faith and Reason* John Paul wrote, 'When God is forgotten the creature itself grows unintelligible.' In par. 90 he went on to say that unbelief, 'makes it possible to erase from the countenance of men and women the marks of their likeness to God and thus leads them little by little either to *a destructive will to power or to a solitude without hope.*' What Popes John Paul and Benedict have said is so true. However, there is often a certain openness to faith present in the experience of contemporary unbelievers.

Psychologists Frankl & Jung on Unbelief

Psychologist Viktor Frankl said that the deepest need of the human heart is meaning of an unconditional kind. When people fail to find such meaning they suffer from what he called 'existential frustration.' He believed that it led to such things as depression, addiction and neurosis. For example, what he refers to as Sunday neurosis is, 'the kind of depression which afflicts people who become aware of a lack of content in their lives when the rush of the busy week is over and the void within them becomes manifest.' He added, 'sometimes the frustrated will to meaning is compensated for by a will to power, including the most primitive form of the will to power, the will to money. In other cases the place of the frustrated will to meaning is taken by the will to pleasure. That is why existential frustration often leads to sexual compensation. We can observe in such cases that the sexual libido becomes rampant in the existential vacuum.'

Psychologist Carl Jung believed that people who are without God and hope are inclined to become neurotic. For example, he wrote, 'In thirty years I have treated many patients in the second half of life [i.e., over 35]. Every one of them became ill because he or she had lost that which the living religions in every age have given their followers, [i.e. religious experience and a sense of ultimate meaning] and none of them was fully healed who did not regain his religious outlook.'

Nostalgia for the Infinite

Pope Paul VI stated in par. 55 of *Evangelisation in the Modern World*, 'one cannot deny the existence of real stepping stones to

Christianity, and of evangelical values at least in the form of a sense of emptiness or nostalgia. It would not be an exaggeration to say that there exists a powerful and tragic appeal to be evangelised.' Pope Francis echoed that sentiment in par. 165 of *The Joy of the Gospel*, 'It is the gospel message which is capable of responding to the desire for the infinite which abides in every human heart.' We will look at four steppingstones that can help to satisfy conscious and unconscious desires for the infinite.

1. Provide a sense of unconditional belonging
Traditionally, as was stated in chapter eighteen, evangelisation involved three things, right *Belief*, right *Behaviour* and a consequent sense of *Belonging*. If the spiritual pilgrims of our day experience, first and foremost, a sense of unconditional belonging within a caring Christian community, they will be more likely to be interested in the Christian beliefs that sustain and inform that community. I recall visiting a parish in Liverpool which was unusually inclusive, the kind of parish that Pope Francis would probably endorse. If you look up St Anne's website you will see that it says that the following type of people are welcome:

- Whatever your experience; divorced/re-married, hurt by the Church, depressed, fearful, unforgiven, or rejected, you are welcome.
- Whatever you wish to leave behind you; alcoholism, paedophilia, child abuse, prostitution, drug pushing, drug addiction, gambling, murder, adultery, wife/husband battering, pornography, abortion, coercing into abortion,

thieving, burglary, vandalism, violence, you are welcome.
- We extend our invitation to whoever you are; young, old, black, white, asylum seeker, immigrant, lesbian, tearaway, rebel, stranger. You too are welcome.
- Whatever your situation; sick, healthy, unmarried, married, co-habiting, single parent, poor, rich, unemployed, employed, homeless, HIV/AIDS, disabled, bereaved, widowed, lapsed Catholic. You are welcome here.

I suspect that one of the reasons why the Alpha course has been so successful in evangelising non-believers is the fact that it creates a sense of unconditional belonging for the spiritual seekers of our day by means of the meal that often precedes the teaching at the meetings and the non-judgemental discussions.

2. Engage in dialogue
Recent Popes have spoken about the need for interreligious dialogue with non-Christian believers and unbelievers. Popes John Paul, Benedict and Francis have talked about it. For example, speaking about such dialogue, Pope Francis said in par. 128 of *The Joy of the Gospel*, 'The first step [to faith] is personal dialogue, when the needy person speaks and shares his or her joys, hopes and concerns for loved ones, or so many other heartfelt needs. Only afterwards is it possible to bring up God's word, perhaps by reading a Bible verse or relating a story, but always keeping in mind the fundamental message: the personal love of God who became man, who gave himself up for us, who is living and who offers us his salvation and his friendship.'

3. Apologetics

Evangelisation as apologetics defends the legitimacy of Christian teaching from the criticisms and misrepresentations of its detractors. At a time when many people are highly educated in all kinds of secular learning there is a need to show how reasonable it is to believe Christian teaching. In his Encyclical *Faith and Reason*, Pope John Paul II has shown how faith and reason strengthen each other. There are many excellent resources of an apologetic nature which are available for use by evangelists. Here are a few examples. *Mere Christianity*, by C. S. Lewis was nominated as the best Christian book of the twentieth century by *Christianity Today* magazine. It has helped many unbelievers to come to faith. Catholic apologists, Peter Kreeft of Boston College, and Scott Hahn of the Franciscan University of Steubenville are also well known for their books on apologetics. Among Protestants, the books of Lee Strobel are also helpful. He has written, *The Case for Faith; The Case for a Creator; & The Case for Christ.* He also has a DVD containing three presentations which are based on his books.

4. Deeds of power

When we welcome people into the Christian community, thereby giving them a sense of unconditional belonging, they may become interested in our personal faith stories which will contain the core Christian beliefs. We can also offer to pray for and with them. If we exercise the charisms of power in doing so they can really help an unbeliever to come to faith in the kerygma. For example, a young man who was an unbeliever came to a Travellers (i.e. Irish gypsies) mission in London in

Jan 2014. He was so impressed by the sense of belonging, the sincere faith of those attending, and the fact that he himself experienced a significant healing, that he decided to become a Catholic and was received into the Church about a year later.

CONCLUSION

Some time ago a well known Italian journalist, Eugene Scalfari, asked Pope Francis whether, unbelievers could be saved. The pontiff responded, 'You ask me if the God of the Christians forgives those who don't believe and who don't seek the faith. I start by saying – and this is the fundamental thing – that God's mercy has no limits if you go to him with a sincere and contrite heart. The issue for those who do not believe in God is to obey their conscience. Sin, even for those who have no faith, exists when people disobey their conscience.'

While that is true, par. 16 of the *Constitution on the Church* of Vatican II indicates that salvation is not easy for unbelievers. It says, 'But often men, deceived by the Evil One, have become vain in their reasonings and have exchanged the truth of God for a lie, serving the creature rather than the Creator.' Ralph Martin has written an excellent book on this topic entitled, *Will Many be Saved? What Vatican II Actually Teaches and its Implications for the New Evangelisation* (Grand Rapids: Eerdmans, 2012). The Lord wants Christians to do their best to evangelise people of this kind, e.g., by such means as friendship evangelisation, person-to-person dialogue, or putting on Alpha Courses which are aimed, principally, at unbelievers.

Suggested questions for reflection and/or discussion

- Would you agree that while St. Paul said that unbelievers are, 'without hope and without God in the world,' it would also be true to say that, either at a conscious or unconscious level, they have, 'a thirst for the infinite'?

- Is it true as Paul VI said that there exists, in unbelievers, 'a powerful and tragic appeal to be evangelised'?

- In your opinion, what are the stepping stones to faith as far as the evangelisation of unbelievers are concerned?

TWENTY ONE

POPE FRANCIS ON EVANGELISING THE LEAST, THE LAST, AND THE LOST

When one reads *The Joy of the Gospel* by Pope Francis, it becomes obvious that, like Jesus, he has a heartfelt concern for the least, the last and the lost. In par. 197 he talks about the fact that Jesus, the evangeliser of the poor, lived as a poor man himself. St. Paul noted, 'For you know the grace of our Lord Jesus Christ, that though he was rich, yet for your sakes he became poor, so that you through his poverty might become rich' (2 Cor 8:9). In the Incarnation the Word divested himself of his divine glory to be born as a vulnerable baby in the poverty of the stable of Bethlehem. Surely it was significant that the first people who came to show him honour were the shepherds, poor people who the Scribes and Pharisees would have thought of as cursed. So, already in this story there is an intimation that Jesus had come to bring Good News to the poor. As his mother said in a prophetic way, 'He has lifted up the humble. He has filled the hungry with good things but has sent the rich away empty' (Lk 1:52-53). In par. 197, Pope Francis also highlights the fact that Jesus made a preferential option for the poor.

St. Luke tells us that Jesus came to Nazareth shortly after his baptism in the Jordan. On the Sabbath he took part in the weekly liturgy. As a lay man noted for learning and piety, he was invited to choose a reading from the prophets and to comment on it. He solemnly and deliberately chose to read from Is 61:1-2 which foretold how the messiah would bring Good News to the poor (cf. Lk 4:18-19). Then we are told, 'he rolled up the scroll, gave it back to the attendant and sat down. The eyes of everyone in the synagogue were fastened on him, and he began by saying to them, 'Today this scripture is fulfilled in your hearing' (Lk 4: 20-21). As was pointed out in chapter six, this was Jesus' mission statement, his solemn declaration of purpose. In Luke 6:20, Jesus spoke to those who lacked material possessions, 'Blessed are you who are poor,' he declared, 'for yours is the kingdom of God.' In Mt 5:3 the words of Jesus were addressed to those who were suffering from an inward sense of deprivation, 'Blessed are the poor in spirit,' he announced, 'for theirs is the kingdom of heaven.' In chapter six we looked at the traditional New Testament understanding of poverty.

CONTEMPORARY POVERTY

Speaking mainly about poverty of a material kind proposition 31 of the post-synodal document *The New Evangelisation for the Transmission of the Christian Faith* said, 'Today there are new poor and new faces of poverty: the hungry, the homeless, the sick and abandoned, drug addicts, migrants and the marginalised, political and environmental refugees, the indigenous peoples. The current economic crisis seriously affects the poor. Among the poorest in contemporary society are the victims of grievous loss of respect for the inviolable dignity of innocent human life.' Not surprisingly, Pope Francis has a lot to say about evangelisation of and by the poor, notably in pars 186-216 of *The Joy of the Gospel*. For the sake of clarity and brevity I am going to highlight just four points that he makes. There are others, I know, but we will focus on these.

A. The Kerygma and the poor

From the start, when a person heard and accepted the Kerygma in faith, he or she would go on to seek and grasp its social implications. The person would see how the gift of God's merciful love would have knock-on effects on his or her conduct and treatment of others, especially the poor. In par. 177, Pope Francis said, 'The kerygma has a clear social content: at the very heart of the Gospel is life in community and engagement with others. The content of the first proclamation has an immediate moral implication centred on charity.' In par. 187 he added, 'Each individual Christian and every community is called to be an instrument of God for the liberation and promotion of the poor, and for enabling them to be fully a part of society.' In chapter six I suggested that following the revelation of the merciful love of Jesus Christ, Christians are called to proclaim and demonstrate that merciful love to the poor of our day, especially those on the margins and periphery of society.

B. Spiritual care of the poor

In par. 200 Pope Francis has these striking words to share, 'I want to say, with regret, that the worst discrimination which the poor suffer is the lack of spiritual care. The great majority of the poor have a special openness to the faith; they need God and we must not fail to offer them his friendship, his blessing, his word, the celebration of the sacraments and a journey of growth and maturity in the faith. Our preferential option for the poor must mainly translate into a privileged and preferential religious care.' Although it is important that the poor are helped in material ways, and that people fight for their rights, it is not enough. Their spiritual needs cannot be neglected. And to help satisfy those needs is an integral part of the new evangelisation. The success of the Alpha Course in prisons is an example of this kind of spiritual care. I know that those who conduct such courses also try to provide spiritual and practical care for ex-prisoners in order to ease their way back into society. It is a big challenge for all of us. What in practical terms can we do to help the poor, those on the margins of contemporary society in a spiritual way?

Pope Francis maintains that while we have to evangelise the poor, we in our turn will be evangelised by them. As he says in par. 198, 'They have much to teach us. Not only do they share in the *sensus fidei* (sense of faith), but in their difficulties they know the suffering Christ. We need to let ourselves be evangelised by them. The new evangelisation is an invitation to acknowledge the saving power at work in their lives and to put them at the centre of the Church's pilgrim way. We are called to find Christ in them, to lend our voice to their causes, but also to be their friends, to listen to them, to speak for them and to embrace the mysterious wisdom which God wishes to share with us through them.' Pope Francis believes that preaching the Good News is not enough. Its message of mercy and love needs to be expressed in deeds of mercy and action for justice.

C. Deeds of mercy

One way of expressing the love of Christ is to have a heart for the poor and to respond with compassion to their needs. In par. 193 Pope Francis refers to the teaching of scripture in this regard, 'The wisdom literature sees almsgiving as a concrete exercise of mercy towards those in need: 'Almsgiving delivers from death, and it will purge away every sin' (Tob 12:9). The idea is expressed even more graphically, 'Water extinguishes blazing fire: so almsgiving atones for sin' (Sir 3:30). The same synthesis appears in the New Testament: 'Maintain constant love for one another, for love covers a multitude of sins' (1 Pet 4:8). This truth greatly influenced the thinking of the Fathers of the Church and helped create a prophetic, counter-cultural resistance to the self-centred hedonism of paganism.'

When I was living in a parish a few years ago one of my colleagues was outstanding in this regard. He seemed to know all the homeless in our area. On Christmas day he rarely attended the Christmas dinner because he was going around the area with lay people in order to bring Christmas dinner to those living on the streets. I also discovered that he had a scheme whereby ex-prisoners and homeless young people could do gardening in order to produce flowers and vegetables for sale. The project brought in a surprisingly large sum of money which was paid out to the young people. There are many organisations such as the Vincent de Paul Society and the Simon Community which express the love of Jesus by doing similar deeds of mercy.

C. Action for justice

In chapter twenty one on conversion of parish structures I point to the fact that Pope Francis talks a lot about the need for systemic changes which will enable structures to be better able to express the missionary impulse. It is much the same when it comes to the poor. It is not enough to tell the poor that God loves them, we have to work hard to lessen the burden of injustice that so often weighs them down. We need to identify the unjust structures of society and do what we can to change them. In par. 194 the Pope speaks a cautionary word to conservative Catholics when he says, 'We should not be concerned simply about falling into doctrinal error, but about remaining faithful to this light-filled path of life and wisdom. For 'defenders of orthodoxy are sometimes accused of passivity, indulgence, or culpable complicity regarding the intolerable situations of injustice and the political regimes which prolong them.'

The Pope insists on putting people before profit. He explains in par. 199, 'The poor person, when loved, 'is esteemed as of great value,' and this is what makes the authentic option for the poor differ from any other ideology, from any attempt to exploit the poor for one's own personal or political interest.' Clearly Pope Francis is neither a Marxist or Peronist, rather he is influenced by the Church's traditional social teaching. In par. 202 Francis says, 'As long as the problems of the poor are not radically resolved by rejecting the absolute autonomy of markets and financial speculation and by attacking the structural causes of inequality, no solution will be found for the world's problems or, for that matter, to any problems. Inequality is the root of social ills.' In par. 204 he adds, 'We can no longer trust in the unseen forces and the invisible hand of the market. Growth in justice requires more than economic growth, while presupposing such growth: it requires decisions, programmes, mechanisms and processes specifically geared to a better distribution of income, the creation of sources of employment and an integral promotion of the poor which goes beyond a simple welfare mentality.'

In Ireland and Britain there are people and groups who are struggling to change things along the lines the Pope suggests, such as the Vincent de Paul Society. In Ireland, it commissions research into injustices and makes yearly submissions at budget time which propose changes. Fr. Peter McVerry, S.J., of the Peter McVerry Trust is much respected as an advocate on behalf of the homeless. In Italy I met an impressive woman called Chiara Amirante founder of the Community of the New Horizons. She told me that she learned her English in Dublin and ministered to people on the streets in the city. Although her community is dedicated to the new evangelisation, a great deal of its work focuses on the poor and the homeless. This is so because Chiara began her evangelistic work by talking to poor people outside Termini train station in Rome. Soon afterwards she gave up her job and decided to work full time for street people. To that end, she came up with the idea of a community to take people in, where the only rule was to try to live out the Gospel. Nowadays, New Horizons has over 207 shelters and education centres. They have even expanded beyond Italy to Brazil. I know that the Pope is a great admirer of what she does. I think he sees her ministry as an example of what he has in mind in *The Joy of the Gospel*.

Conclusion

Those of us who are dedicated to primary evangelisation by proclaiming the kerygma are not used to the way of thinking which the Pope proposes with regard to the poor. As was pointed out in chapter two the Pope's approach is characteristic of the political/developmental model of evangelisation. In chapter three, it was mentioned that action for justice is integral to a holistic view of evangelisation. What Pope Francis says in *The Joy of the Gospel* and later in *On Care of our Common Home*, 222-227 is very challenging. For example, in par. 222 he says, 'Christian spirituality proposes an alternative understanding of the quality of life, and encourages a prophetic and contemplative lifestyle, one capable of deep enjoyment free of the obsession with consumption. We need to take up an ancient lesson, found in different religious traditions and also in the Bible. It is the conviction that 'less is more.'

Suggested questions for reflection and/or discussion

- When Jesus talked about 'the poor' and the 'poor in spirit,' who exactly was he talking about? Who are the poor in today's world?

- Clearly Pope Francis thinks that action for justice and liberation from social and economic oppression is an integral part of evangelisation. What does he mean by saying that evangelisers have to work to bring about systemic change in society?

- Would you agree with Pope Francis when he says, that 'the worst discrimination which the poor suffer is the lack of spiritual care'?

TWENTY TWO

HOLINESS, WITNESS AND EVANGELISATION

Second Vatican Council said that all the faithful, clerical and lay, share in two interrelated vocations of a universal nature, namely the calls to holiness and evangelisation. As John Paul II said in par. 90 of *Mission of the Redeemer*, 'The universal call to to holiness is closely linked to the universal call to mission. Every member of the faithful is called to holiness and to mission. This was the earnest desire of the Council. The Church's missionary spirituality is a journey towards holiness.' Clearly there is a reciprocal relationship between holiness and evangelisation. Holiness is not really possible without evangelisation, and effective evangelisation is not really possible without holiness.

THE NATURE OF HOLINESS

A number of years ago I was asked to drive Cardinal Mc Cann of Capetown in South Africa to visit Cardinal Thomas O' Fee in Armagh, Northern Ireland. On the way back I asked the prelate if he had attended the Second Vatican Council. He told me, in no uncertain terms, that indeed he had. Then I asked him what had impressed him most about the council. Without hesitation, he replied, 'Fr. Collins the thing that impressed me most about the Council was the universal call to holiness. It is addressed not only to priests and religious, it is also addressed to the laity in virtue of their baptismal incorporation into Christ.' For some strange reason his words made a big impression on me. As a result, I gave much thought to the question, what is holiness? I came to the tentative conclusion that it was the result of three things:

- Being filled with the Spirit (cf. Eph 5:18)
- Guided by the Spirit (cf. Gal: 5:18)
- Empowered by the Spirit (cf. Phil 2:13)

A. Filled with the Spirit

The subject of being filled with the Spirit was dealt with in chapter nine. Of course, being filled with God's merciful love is not a one off event. Rather it initiates a lifelong process whereby the reception of God's Spirit can be deepened and strengthened day by day.

B. Guided by the Spirit

At the heart of St. Paul's ethics was the injunction, 'be guided by the Spirit so that in all things you may do the will of God' (Gal 5:18). Talking about God's will in a generalised way, St. Paul said, 'the commandments, 'Do not commit adultery,' 'Do not murder,' 'Do not steal,' 'Do not covet,' and whatever other commandment there may be, are summed up in this one rule: 'Love your neighbour as yourself.' Love does no harm to its neighbour. Therefore love is the fulfilment of the law' (Rm 13:9-10). Paul appreciated that one needed a spirit of wisdom and revelation to discover the nuances of God's will, so he disclosed, 'we have not stopped praying for you and asking God to fill you with the knowledge of his will through all spiritual wisdom and understanding. And we pray this in order that you may live a life worthy of the Lord and may please him in every way' (Col 1:9-10). I have written a book on this subject entitled, *Guided by God: Ordinary and Charismatic Ways of Discovering God's Will* (Luton: New life, 2015).

C. Empowered by the Spirit

In Jn 15:5 Jesus said that 'apart from me you can do nothing.' St. Paul learned this truth in no uncertain terms when he asked God to remove some secret thorn from his flesh. The Lord declined to do so while declaring, 'My grace is sufficient for you, for my power is made perfect in weakness' (2 Cor 12:9). On another occasion Paul said, 'I can do everything through him who gives me strength' (Phil 4:13). In Phil 2:13, he wrote, 'it is God who works in you to will and to act according to his good purpose' (Phil 2:13). Speaking about the power at work within him Paul said, 'That power is like the working of his mighty strength, which he exerted in Christ when he raised him from the dead and seated him at his right hand in the heavenly realms' (Eph 1:19-20).

The extent to which a Christian is filled, guided and empowered by the Spirit, in his or her daily life, is the extent to which he or she will be holy. Some time ago I received what I thought was a prophetic word from the Lord. Part of it said, 'Be holy as I am holy. There is no substitute for this holiness. There is no plan, effort or activity, no matter how well intentioned, which will accomplish my purposes if you are not holy like Me.'

Holiness and witness

There is an interesting passage in the first letter of Peter where he talks about the way in which believing wives can win over their unbelieving husbands to the faith. He said, 'be submissive to your husbands so that, if any of them do not believe the word, they may be won over without words by the behaviour of their wives, when they see the purity and reverence of your lives' (1 Pt 3:1-5).

It is interesting to note that the earliest Irish manuscript still extant is the *Cambrai Homily*. It was written in old Irish around the seventh century A.D. It deals with three kinds of wordless witness or martyrdom, white, green and red:

- People experience *white* martyrdom when they separate from everything that they love for God, (e.g., leaving kith and kin to go overseas on mission).
- People undergo *green* martyrdom when, as a result of fasting and penance they control their worldly desires in order to become more Christ like.
- People suffer *red* martyrdom when they shed their blood and die for Christ's sake.

Recent Popes have reiterated those teachings

- Pope Paul VI said in par. 41 of *Evangelisation in the Modern World*, 'the first means of evangelisation is the witness of an authentically Christian life, given over to God in a communion that nothing should destroy and at

the same time given to one's neighbour with limitless zeal. As we said recently to a group of lay people, modern man listens more willingly to witnesses than to teachers, and if he does listen to teachers, it is because they are witnesses.'
- Pope John Paul said something very similar in par. 42 of *Mission of the Redeemer*, 'People today,' he said, 'put more trust in witnesses than in teachers, in experience than in teaching, and in life and action than in theories. The witness of a Christian life is the first and irreplaceable form of mission.'

Surely, Fr. Werenfried van Straaten, the founder of the charity Aid to the Church in Need, was correct when he said in a homily for Pentecost, 'The Gospel has been printed millions of times on paper. It is sold in all languages. But people, nowadays do not ask for a paper Gospel. They demand a living Gospel. They hunger for Christ who is the living Good News. They are waiting to meet men and women in whom Christ becomes visible again, in whom they can recognise and love Christ. They demand of us that we should give Christ a living form again.' Fr. van Straaten's words were reminiscent of what St. Paul said in 2 Cor 3:2-3, 'You yourselves are our letter, written on your hearts, known and read by everybody. You show that you are a letter from Christ, the result of our ministry, written not with ink but with the Spirit of the living God, not on tablets of stone but on tablets of human hearts.'

Here are just a few examples of what typically happens in the more humdrum circumstances of everyday life, when Christians are filled, guided and empowered by the Spirit:

- Employees are chatting during a coffee break. Not only are they taking the Holy Name of Jesus in vain and using profane language, they also begin to tell dirty jokes. However, a conscientious Christian refuses to join in.
- Young people go on holidays together to Spain. They arrange to sleep together, but one Christian girl declines the offer because she doesn't intend having sex until she is married.
- A group of friends are bad mouthing and criticising a person they know, but one of them not only says nothing negative about the person in question, she actually draws attention to good points in that person's character.
- A man buys a new suit in a tailor's shop. He pays by cash and finds that he has been given too much in change. He draws the attention of the cashier to the mistake and hands the money back.
- A family have fallen on hard times in the parish, they have a daughter who needs an expensive operation. An anonymous donor sends a substantial sum of money in the post with a typed note which says that he is praying to the Lord for the girl's recovery.
- There is an anti-abortion rally and hundreds of Catholics protest with dignity outside Government Buildings on a cold, rainy day.
- A widow hears about a recovering drug addict who can't find anywhere to live. She offers to take the girl into her home. The addict remains with the widow for four months during which time she feeds her guest and often listens to the sad story of her life.

- A young man knows that L'Arche are looking for volunteers who will live with handicapped adults. He offers his services for six months.

Surely Cardinal Suhard (1874-1949) was correct when he said, 'The great mark of a Christian is what no other characteristic can replace, namely, the example of a life that can only be explained in terms of God (in Christ).'

HOLINESS AND WITNESS ARE NOT SUFFICIENT

There is a saying, which is incorrectly attributed to St. Francis of Assisi, which says, 'Go into all the world and preach the gospel, and, if necessary, use words.' The truth is, while personal and community witness to the truth of the Gospel of mercy and love is essential, it is not enough. The Good News has to be proclaimed in words as well.

- In par. 44 of *The Mission of the Redeemer,* Pope John Paul II wrote, 'Evangelisation will always contain - as the foundation, centre and at the same time the summit of its dynamism - a clear proclamation that, in Jesus Christ... salvation is offered to all people, as a gift of God's grace and mercy.'
- Echoing the words of John Paul II, Pope Francis said in par. 110 of *The Joy of the Gospel,* 'there can be no true evangelisation without the explicit proclamation of Jesus as Lord,' and without 'the primacy of the proclamation of Jesus Christ in all evangelising work.'

Jesus brought the interrelated notions of proclamation and witness together when he said, 'Do not believe me unless I do what my Father does. But if I do it, even though you do not believe me, believe the miracles (Jn 10:37-38). When one's actions fail to match one's words, such hypocrisy is counter-productive.

Suggested question for reflection and/or discussion

- Do you think that the gap between what Christians profess and what they do, can be an obstacle to effective evangelisation?

- What in your opinion is the meaning of holiness? Who epitomises that holiness for you? Why?

- Would you agree that while credible witness is vital, it is not sufficient where evangelisation is concerned?

TWENTY THREE

BUILDING A MISSIONARY DIOCESE

As we all know, the notion of conversion is a key Christian concept. Needless to say a personal understanding of conversion is both valid and important. However, in proposition 22 of the 2012 Synod of Bishops on *The New Evangelisation for the Transmission of the Christian Faith* a second understanding of conversion was mentioned, one which is very relevant where any diocese and its parishes are concerned. Having stated that, 'The New Evangelisation requires personal and communal conversion,' it went on to add, 'The New Evangelisation guides us to an authentic pastoral conversion which moves us to attitudes and initiatives which lead to evaluations and changes in the dynamics of pastoral structures which no longer respond to the evangelical demands of the current time.'

When one reads *The Joy of the Gospel* it is clear that Pope Francis talks mainly about conversion in these structural terms, as the call to change the ways in which the diocese and its parishes are organised in order to make them better able to carry out their missionary mandate. In par. 26 of *The Joy of the Gospel*, the Pontiff stated, 'The Second Vatican Council presented ecclesial conversion as openness to a constant self-renewal born of fidelity to Jesus Christ.' In par. 27 Francis added that the call to evangelise would be the main criterion that would determine what structural changes were needed:

- The Church's customs
- Ways of doing things
- Times and schedules
- Language and structures

They can be suitably channelled for the evangelisation of today's world rather than for her self-preservation.'

If they are acted on, these words could have revolutionary implications for our dioceses and parishes. As Pope John Paul II said in par 2 of the *Mission of the Redeemer* 'There is a new awareness that missionary activity is for all Christians, for all dioceses and parishes.' Would it not be true to say that, as they are currently constituted, our dioceses and parishes are not yet sufficiently outward looking and missionary. Where dioceses are concerned a number of things can usefully be done.

A. An office of evangelisation

Firstly, each one of them needs to have an office of evangelisation. That office needs to have a director and an evangelisation team which seeks to promote local initiatives for the New Evangelisation in practical ways. Speaking about the aims of its office for evangelisation one American diocese states that it,

- 'Assists parishes in implementing programmes for

evangelisation through various approved ecclesial movements;
- includes ongoing faith development for Catholics;
- reaches out to inactive and alienated Catholics, and those with no church affiliation.'

B. A Diocesan evangelisation team

Secondly, the office of evangelisation needs to set up a diocesan evangelisation team which might contain one or two priests and a number of lay people from around the diocese who have a heart for the new evangelisation and know something about it. The team should take note of what John Paul II said in par 29 of *At the Beginning of the New Millennium,* 'It is in the local churches that the specific features of a detailed pastoral plan can be identified, goals and methods, formation and enrichment of the people involved, the search for the necessary resources, which will enable the proclamation of Christ to reach people, mould communities, and have a deep and incisive influence in bringing Gospel values to bear in society and culture.' Let's look at what the Pope said in a little more detail:

Firstly, there is need for a pastoral plan. Christian leaders, like Nehemiah of old, need to have a vision that has been revealed to them by God and not discovered by merely human effort. As the King James version of the Bible puts it, 'Where there is no vision, the people perish' The vision of the diocesan evangelisation team should find expression in a mission statement. Having a such a statement enables the diocesan evangelisation outreach to be proactive by focusing on evangelistic priorities rather than reacting to all kinds of pressing pastoral needs. Without a mission statement the diocesan team is in danger of being like a rudderless ship. I'm firmly convinced that a diocese that focuses on the satisfaction of urgent pastoral needs to the exclusion of evangelistic priorities contributes by default to the demise of the church.

Secondly, establish a few realistic goals which will give concrete expression to the vision, expressed in the mission statement, and state what action steps will be required to achieve those goals. For example, the diocesan evangelisation team might agree that formation for evangelisation is required in the diocese. In this connection we looked at what the Church has to say about it in the introduction to this book.

In 2008 four of us of us set up The New Springtime Community in Dublin. Speaking about formation for evangelisation our mission statement said, 'we will put on practical courses that will teach lay people about the nature, motives and means of engaging in the new evangelisation.' To this end we designed a six session long *Parish Evangelisation Course*, and a certificate course which includes 26 sessions. This book grew from those lectures. We also produce teaching materials such as CDs and books on evangelisation. These are the kind of things that an evangelisation team can organise in any diocese. I would recommend that dioceses think about setting up a school of evangelisation. As was mentioned in the introduction to this book, proposition 46 of the 2012 post synodal document, *The New Evangelisation for the Transmission of the Christian Faith* says,

'This Synod considers that it is necessary to establish formation centers for the New Evangelisation, where lay people learn how to speak of the person of Christ in a persuasive manner adapted to our time and to specific groups of people, e.g., young adults, agnostics, the elderly and so forth.'

Thirdly, the diocesan evangelisation team need to look for resources that will enable parishes to carry out their evangelising mission.

- Get good people on to the archdiocesan team, who have education/training in new evangelisation. Make sure to have some young adults on the team. If necessary encourage them to up-skill by doing a course, e.g., at Maryvale in Birmingham, England which has a number of good correspondence courses available such as, Certificates in Evangelisation and Ministry; Evangelisation and Ministry for Youth; Evangelisation and Ministry for the Parish; and Evangelisation and Ministry for the Family.
- Finances are also necessary in order to resource evangelisation. For example, in Alpha Ireland we have employed a financial director who raises funds for our operations such as running an office, paying a full time coordinator and three full time youth directors who work with secondary school students. The cost is well over 100,000 euro a year.
- Draw up and publish an evangelisation directory which lists all the groups that are engaged in evangelisation in and outside the diocese, with a brief

description of what they have to offer, together with relevant information such as contact people, postal addresses, phone numbers, email addresses, and websites.
- Be willing to have members of the diocesan evangelising team visit parishes to facilitate their pastoral councils in reflecting on evangelisation, and to give practical advice when it is sought.

Conclusion

As we in the contemporary church hear the call to structural conversion we often resist because we find that it can be unsettling, demanding and painful. Bl. John Henry Newman was right when he said, 'To live is to change, and to be perfect is to have changed often.' On occasions we try to rationalise our unwillingness to co-operate by offering spurious reasons for remaining in our comfort zones. In reality our resistance is probably rooted in selfishness, a lack of generosity and fear, none of which are inspired by the Holy Spirit. We end this chapter with some words of Pope Francis from par 33 of the *Joy of the Gospel*, 'Pastoral ministry in a missionary key seeks to abandon the complacent attitude that says: 'We have always done it this way.' I invite everyone [including dioceses] to be bold and creative in this task of rethinking the goals, structures, style and methods of evangelisation in their respective communities. A proposal of goals without an adequate communal search for the means of achieving them will inevitably prove illusory.'

SUGGESTED QUESTIONS FOR REFLECTION AND/OR DISCUSSION

- What was the most helpful idea you noticed in this chapter? Why so?

- In your opinion what changes are required in your diocese in order to promote the new evangelisation?

- How can the diocese help your parish to become more missionary?

TWENTY FOUR

CONVERSION OF PARISH STRUCTURES AND THE NEW EVANGELISATION

In spite of all the problems they face, such as clergy shortage, clustering and fluctuacting membership, modern parishes are still the focal point of the new evangelisation. In proposition 44 of the 2012 Synod of bishops on *The New Evangelisation for the Transmission of the Christian Faith* we read, 'The parish, in and through all of its activities, should animate its members to become agents of the New Evangelisation, witnessing through both their words and their lives' Speaking about the nature of the parish Pope Francis said in par. 28 of *The Joy of the Gospel*, 'In all its activities the parish encourages and trains its members to be evangelisers. It is a community of communities, a sanctuary where the thirsty come to drink in the midst of their journey, and a centre of constant missionary outreach. We must admit, though, that the call to review and renew our parishes has not yet sufficed to bring them nearer to people, to make them environments of living communion and participation, and to make them completely mission-oriented.'

In recent years many of those who have written about evangelisation in the parish have asked the question, are the structures of the parish more devoted to maintenance than to mission? It is clear that Pope Francis identifies with that question. In par. 25 he said, 'I hope that all communities will devote the necessary effort to advancing along the path of a pastoral and missionary conversion which cannot leave things as they presently are. Mere administration can no longer be enough. Throughout the world, let us be permanently in a state of mission.' In par. 27 he quoted some words which John Paul II had addressed to the bishops of Oceania, 'All renewal in the Church must have mission as its goal if it is not to fall prey to a kind of ecclesial introversion.'

STRUCTURES SHOULD FACILITATE EVANGELISATION
In par. 26 Francis observed that, 'There are ecclesial structures which can hamper efforts at evangelisation, yet even good structures are only helpful when there is a life constantly driving, sustaining and assessing them. Without new life and an authentic evangelical spirit, without the Church's 'fidelity to her own calling,' any new structure will soon prove ineffective.' So not surprisingly he said in par. 33 of *The Joy of the Gospel*, 'Pastoral ministry in a missionary key seeks to abandon the complacent attitude that says: 'We have always done it this way.' I invite everyone to be bold and creative in this task of rethinking the goals, structures, style and methods of evangelisation in their respective communities. A proposal of goals without an adequate communal search for the means of achieving them will inevitably prove illusory.'

Here is a checklist of questions which are designed to establish whether a parish is missionary in its orientation or not.
   1. Has the parish a mission statement, one that includes an explicit commitment to evangelisation?

2. Does the parish have a yearly plan that states what individuals and groups will do to evangelise the un-churched in the area, and how they will do it?
3. Does the parish have any form of outreach to the unbelievers within its territory?
4. What does the parish do to evangelise young adults between the ages of 18 and 35?
5. Does the parish council have an evangelisation sub-committee that plans evangelistic activities?
6. Does the parish provide any training for parishioners who want to learn how to evangelise effectively alone and in groups?
7. Is there an evangelisation team in the parish that does house-to-house visitation?
8. If there is an occasional parish mission, is it mainly focused on those who practice or is there a conscious, organised effort to reach out to the un-churched either during or after the mission, e.g., by putting on Alpha Courses?
9. Does the parish newsletter contain regular articles to do with the nature of evangelisation, the motives parishioners have of engaging in it, and practical means of doing so?
10. Are there any groups in the parish, such as the housebound, or an intercessory prayer group, who are praying in an intentional way for parish renewal and evangelisation in the area?
11. If people are evangelised, are there any groups they can join which would give them a sense of belonging and help with their on-going formation? Examples of faith

nurturing groups would be Lectio Divina Groups, Pastorates, Parish Cell Groups, Prayer Groups etc.

If a parish cannot answer yes to at least six of these questions, it probably means that it is too inward looking. Unfortunately, there would be nothing unusual in that. It would probably be true to say that most Catholic parishes are better at shepherding the people who still attend church, than fishing for the majority of those who no longer attend. Not surprisingly, although Francis advocates the need for structural changes which facilitate missionary activity, obviously he cannot specify what changes are needed in individual parishes because of their different circumstances. Speaking about the current situation the Pope says par. 28 of *The Joy of the Gospel*, 'We must admit, though, that the call to review and renew our parishes has not yet sufficed to bring them nearer to people, to make them environments of living communion and participation, and to make them completely mission-oriented.'

AN EXAMPLE OF BEST PRACTICE
When I was living in Detroit I heard Fr. Mark Montminy of St. Marie's in Manchester, New Hampshire, tell the story of how his struggling inner-city parish had been transformed from being a dispirited, introspective community to being a more outgoing, and evangelising one. Mark himself had undergone a spiritual awakening when he experienced the power of the kerygma as a result of attending a *Cursillo* weekend and sometime later he was baptised in the Holy Spirit as a result of attending a Life in the Spirit Seminar. He said that when he

arrived in St. Marie's parish, the pastoral council, like so many others, was reacting to urgent needs while neglecting pastoral and evangelistic priorities. They were preoccupied with administrative issues such as the purchase of new boilers, reducing the parish debt, fixing a leak in the church roof and the like.

Fr. Mark met with the parish pastoral council and invited them to pray for an outpouring of the Spirit and to dream prayerfully with him about the future of the parish. For the next five months each meeting began with an hour of prayer and afterwards by sharing dreams of what the parish could look like in five and ten years time. Fr. Montminy put the primary emphasis on the need to discover a God given vision for the parish and its future. Eventually, the parishioners expressed that vision in these words, 'Today, in the midst of a disintegrating society marked by alienation, loneliness and despair, we feel a particular urgency to rekindle and magnify the power of our Beacon; for only the Light of Christ can overcome the darkness of this present age and only his love can bring us fullness of life. As we continue our journey with God, we will keep our eyes on the cross of Christ, our ears attentive to His Word, and our hearts docile to His Spirit. In that same Spirit we offer what follows as a means through which God's plan for our community is fulfilled.'

Encouraged by Fr. Mark, St. Marie's parish pastoral council also organised a meeting where any and every parishioner, who so wished, could speak about their hopes for the future. Following this process the pastoral council attempted to compose a mission statement in collaboration with every existing committee, society and organisation in the parish. Finally, they published the following mission statement. 'That all who join St. Marie Parish may come to know Jesus Christ in a more personal way, to accept Him as their Lord and Saviour, and to be His Light in the world, proclaiming the Good News in word and deed. We will do this:

- By providing a Eucharistic liturgy marked by living faith, prophetic preaching and inspiring music, in the midst of a welcoming environment.
- By emphasising the power of prayer - both in community and in the silence of hearts as a source of strength and nourishment for our spiritual journey.
- By offering catechetical programs which will lead people to a deepened understanding of our faith.
- By promoting social justice as a community through financial means and personal sacrifice and through community programs.
- By being an evangelising community who reach out with the Gospel to families, friends and co-workers, and who welcome in our midst all those who seek Jesus; the Way, the Truth and the Life.'

It strikes me that this is not only a really inspiring mission statement, it is one that aims to change parish structures in order to make them more missionary in orientation.

Although Fr. Mark Montminy was clearly a gifted leader in his parish, the willingness to change their thinking and practices was shared by the community and expressed through the parish pastoral council together with the parish priest. His journey is recounted in 'The Story of an Evangelising Parish' in *John Paul II and the New Evangelisation,* edited by Ralph Martin and Peter Williamson. Since then two other inspiring accounts of parish renewal have been published. The first was written by Fr. Michael White and Tom Corcoran. It is entitled, *Rebuilt: Awakening the Faithful, Reaching the Lost, and Making Church Matter.* It describes how the parish of the Nativity in Baltimore, USA, was transformed to become missionary as a result of good leadership. Another book by Fr James Mallon, entitled, *Divine Renovation: Bringing Your Parish from Maintenance to Mission* tells a similarly inspiring story of transformation.

CONCLUSION

As early as 1991 the American bishops produced an excellent document entitled, *Go and Make Disciples.* In par. 85 it said, 'Every element of the parish must respond to the evangelical imperative priests, religious, lay persons, parish staff, ministers, organisations, social clubs, local schools and parish religious education programmes. Otherwise evangelisation will be something a few people in the parish see as their ministry rather than the reason for the parish's existence *and the objective of every ministry in the parish.'* I suspect that we have a long way to go before we achieve that goal. It will require personal and structural conversion. In pages 158-175 of *Basic Evangelisation: Guidelines for Catholics* (Dublin: Columba, 2010) I have made suggestions about possible ways in which parishes can make structural changes which would facilitate the new evangelisation.

Suggested questions for reflection and/or discussion

- In your opinion can the notion of individuals being converted be extended to include the conversion of parish structures?

- What structures in your parish could be changed in order to facilitate evangelisation by the parishioners?

- Why do parishes resist the call to structural conversion?

TWENTY FIVE

THE HOMILY AND THE NEW EVANGELISATION

Pope John Paul II observed in par. 6 of his encyclical *Church of the Eucharist*, 'To contemplate Christ involves being able to recognise him wherever he manifests himself, in his many forms of presence, but above all in the living sacrament of his body and his blood.....Whenever the Church celebrates the Eucharist, the faithful can in some way relive the experience of the two disciples on the road to Emmaus: 'their eyes were opened and they recognised him' (Lk 24:31). When one examines the text in Lk 24:13-35 it becomes apparent that it refers to four presences of Christ which are mentioned in par. 7 of the *Constitution of the Sacred Liturgy* of the Second Vatican Council.

- Christ is present in the gathering of the people.
- Christ is present in the priest who presides.
- Christ is present in the readings from Scripture and in the homily..
- Christ is sacramentally present in the consecrated bread and wine.

This chapter is going to focus on the third form of presence in the word of God, especially in the homily.

WHAT IS A HOMILY?

There is a need to distinguish between sermons and homilies. When I was ordained the very first parish mass I was asked to celebrate was in a church near the seminary. On that occasion I gave a sermon on the truth that the Church is holy. It was one of a sequence of catechetical instructions which the Archbishop of our diocese had instructed us to preach. My sermon had nothing to do with the readings of the day. In contrast, a homily is a talk based on the liturgical readings which explains what the sacred authors intended to say and suggests how their message relates, in a practical way, to life as it is lived today. Apparently, Protestant theologian Karl Barth once said, 'Take your Bible and take your newspaper, and read both. But interpret newspapers from the perspective of your Bible.' Pope Benedict spoke about relating the scripture text to everyday life when he said in par. 59 of on the *Word of God*, 'The homily is part of the liturgical action and is meant to foster a deeper understanding of the word of God, so that it can bear fruit in the lives of the faithful... For this reason preachers need to be in close and constant contact with the sacred text; they should prepare for the homily by meditation and prayer, so as to preach with conviction and passion.' It could also be said that it is easier to preach ten homilies than to live one of them.

PREPARING TO WRITE A HOMILY

Some clergy maintain that they are so busy that usually they don't have the time to engage in the hours of *lectio divina* and scripture study that homily preparation requires. Pope Francis responded in par. 146 of *The Joy of the Gospel* where he wrote,

'To interpret a biblical text, we need to be patient, to put aside all other concerns, and to give it our time, interest and undivided attention. We must leave aside any other pressing concerns and create an environment of serene concentration.' The Pope goes on to say in par. 145 of *The Joy of the Gospel*, 'Some pastors argue that time consuming preparation is not possible given the vast number of tasks which they must perform; nonetheless, I presume to ask that each week a sufficient portion of personal and community time be dedicated to this task, even if less time has to be given to other important activities.' This advice distinguishes between pastoral *needs* and evangelistic *priorities*. I'm convinced that the bishop, priest or deacon who focuses on the satisfaction of urgent pastoral needs to the exclusion of evangelical priorities, such as homily preparation, contributes by default to the decline of the Church.

Members of the clergy need to make time in order to prepare their homilies well. Otherwise they will disappoint themselves and the people. As Pope Francis says in par. 135 of *The Joy of the Gospel*, 'We know that the faithful attach great importance to the homily, and that both they and their ordained ministers suffer because of homilies: the laity from having to listen to them and the clergy from having to preach them! It is sad that this is the case. The homily can actually be an intense and happy experience of the Spirit, a consoling encounter with God's word, a constant source of renewal and growth.' Clergy need to make time for prayer and study so as to prepare good homilies.

A. Prayer

Speaking to the International Congress commemorating the 40th anniversary of *Word of God* Pope Benedict XVI said, 'The diligent reading of Sacred Scripture accompanied by prayer brings about that intimate dialogue in which the person reading hears God who is speaking, and in praying responds to him with trusting openness of heart. If it is effectively promoted, this practice will bring to the Church - I am convinced of it - a new spiritual springtime.' It is clear that Church documents recommend the use of *lectio divina*. That topic has been explored in chapter eleven. Many priests and deacons have found that if they are members of a parish scripture group that does *lectio divina* on the readings of the following Sunday or feast day, the insights gleaned can be very helpful when it comes time to write a relevant homily.

B. Scripture study

Speaking on this topic Pope Francis says in par. 147 of *The Joy of the Gospel*, 'we need to be sure that we understand the meaning of the words we read. I want to insist here on something which may seem obvious, but which is not always taken into account: the biblical text which we study is two or three thousand years old; its language is very different from that which we speak today. Even if we think we understand the words translated into our own language, this does not mean that we correctly understand what the sacred author wished to say. The different tools provided by literary analysis are well known: attention to words which are repeated or emphasised, recognition of the structure and specific movement of a text, consideration of the role played by the different characters, and so forth.'

In pars 115-118 of the *Catechism of the Catholic Church* we read, 'According to an ancient tradition, one can distinguish between two senses of Scripture: the literal and the spiritual.' The *literal sense* is the meaning conveyed by the words of Scripture and discovered by the historical-critical method which follows rules of sound interpretation. It can be very helpful, in this regard, to use a scholarly version of the Bible such as *The New Jerusalem Bible,* or *The Revised New American Bible* which include a wealth of cross references and explanatory footnotes. Bible commentaries are also very useful, such as *The New Jerome Biblical Commentary.*

SOME CHARACTERISTICS OF A GOOD HOMILY

Recent Popes have had many things to say about the characteristics of good homilies. Here are some of them:

- *Brief.* Homilies should be relatively short. In par. 138 of *The Joy of the Gospel,* Francis says that the homily, 'should be brief and avoid taking on the semblance of a speech or a lecture.' In par. 156 he adds, 'In the Bible, for example, we can find advice on how to prepare a homily so as to best to reach people: 'Speak concisely, say much in few words' (Sir 32:8).'
- *Simple.* Francis advocates simplicity of language. In par. 158, he says, 'Preachers often use words learned during their studies and in specialised settings which are

not part of the ordinary language of their hearers. These are words that are suitable in theology or catechesis, but whose meaning is incomprehensible to the majority of Christians.'

- *Clear.* Speaking about this point Francis says in par. 158, 'We need to ensure that the homily has thematic unity, clear order and correlation between sentences, so that people can follow the preacher easily and grasp his line of argument.'
- *Positive.* Francis believes that homilists should accentuate the positive. In par. 159 he says, 'It is not so much concerned with pointing out what shouldn't be done, but with suggesting what we can do better. . . Positive preaching always offers hope, points to the future, does not leave us trapped in negativity.'
- *Christocentric.* Addressing believers who listen to homilies St Ignatius of Antioch said in par. 9 of his Epistle to the Trallians, in *Early Christian Writings: The Apostolic Fathers* (London: Penguin Classics, 1975), 'Close your ears if anyone preaches to you without speaking of Jesus Christ.' In par 59 of *The Word of God,* Pope Benedict XVI said, 'The faithful should be able to perceive clearly that the preacher has a compelling desire to present Christ, who must stand at the centre of every homily.'
- *Kerygmatic.* As we noted in previous chapters the kerygma is the core teaching of the Christian religion. Speaking about the preacher himself, Pope Francis says in par. 151, 'What is essential is that the preacher be certain that God loves him, that Jesus Christ has saved him and

that his love always has the last word.' In the course of an interview reported in *America* magazine, Sept 30th 2013, Francis said, 'A beautiful homily, a genuine sermon must begin with the first proclamation, with the proclamation of salvation. There is nothing more solid, deep and sure than this proclamation. Then you have to do catechesis. Then you can draw even a moral consequence. But *the proclamation of the saving love of God comes before moral and religious imperatives.*'

- *Pneumatic.* Not surprisingly, the Pope stresses the role of the Holy Spirit when writing and preaching a homily. In par. 151 he writes, 'The Holy Spirit, who inspired the word, today, just as at the beginning of the Church, acts in every evangeliser who allows himself to be possessed and led by him. The Holy Spirit places on his lips the words which he could not find by himself.'
- *Imaginative.* All good communicators appreciate the value of images and examples. Speaking about this, Pope Francis says in par. 157, 'An attractive image makes the message seem familiar, close to home, practical and related to everyday life. A successful image can make people savour the message, awaken a desire and move the will towards the Gospel. A good homily, an old teacher once told me, should have 'an idea, a sentiment, an image.'
- *Personal.* Over the years I have found that one can share personal experiences if they are intended to make sense of the point under consideration, rather than drawing attention to oneself. Needless to say, Pope Francis warns against the tendency to preach oneself rather than

the gospel. In par. 138 he states, 'the words of the preacher must be measured, so that the Lord, more than his minister, will be the centre of attention.'
- Relevant. Pope Francis says that priests should have a knowledge of the people they serve. In a striking image he said, 'be shepherds with the smell of sheep.'
- Prophetic. In a homily on Dec 13th 2013, Pope Francis said, 'Lord, free your people from a spirit of clericalism and aid them with a spirit of prophecy,' Then he added, 'In the heart of a prophet are three different times, the promise of the past, contemplation of the present, and courage to show the way towards the future.' Homilies need to have a prophetic cutting edge. As St. Peter said, 'if anyone speaks, they should do so as one who speaks the very words of God' (1 Pt 4:11). However, there is always the danger that, 'The prophets prophesy lies, the priests rule by their own authority, and my people love it this way' (Jer 5:31). Homilists are called to speak the truth in love, and not to court popularity.

Here are a few points that might be helpful when writing evangelistic homilies.

Writing a Homily

It might sound like an obvious thing to say, but often it is ignored; a good homily has a beginning, middle and an end, which ideally lasts between eight and twelve minutes.

- The beginning aims to introduce the main point of the

homily in a striking way with an image, anecdote, interesting fact etc.
- The explanation of the liturgical readings and their relevance comprises the body of the homily. It is best to focus on one point.
- The conclusion aims to suggest practical ways in which the listeners could respond to the readings.

As a follower of Vincent de Paul, I find that the saint's *Little Method* of preaching is extremely helpful. It consists of three interrelated parts which need to be varied depending on the subject under consideration:

- Firstly, it deals with the *nature* of the subject, e.g. salvation.
- Secondly, the preacher suggests *motives* for acting, e.g., why a person should desire to experience salvation, such as sorrow for offending the Lord, and fear of losing heaven etc.
- Thirdly, the preacher deals with the *means* of doing something practical and specific, e.g., trusting in the free, unmerited gift of God's mercy, and making a good general confession.

Speaking about the *Little Method* Vincent said, that it was the method of Jesus Christ himself. He exclaimed on one occasion, 'Three cheers for simplicity, and for the 'little method' which is in fact, the most excellent method and one that brings more glory because it moves hearts more than all this speech giving which only irritates the listener.'

Suggested questions for reflection and/or reflection

- What was the last homily you heard? Would you think that it was good or bad? Why so?

- If a priest or deacon asked for your advice about homilies, what would you say?

- If you are a priest or deacon, do you think that you give sufficient time to preparing your homilies?

TWENTY SIX

EVANGELISATION COURSES IN THE PARISH

It requires a good deal of conviction and courage to engage in person-to-person evangelisation but it is easier for most Catholics to help in running one or other of the basic evangelisation courses that are currently available. This chapter will look at a number of the better known ones here in Ireland and Britain, such as Life in the Spirit Seminars, Alpha and the Philip Course. I should say that there are a number of other good courses which we will not deal with here. The beauty of these courses is that they are run by a group of parishioners, their dynamics and content are pre-prepared, and they are aimed at different types of people such as,

- Church-goers who are not fully evangelised
- The un-churched, or lapsed.

1. Life in the Spirit Seminars

In chapter one there was mention of a faith crisis of head, heart and hands in the contemporary Church. The Life in the Spirit Seminars, which were devised by the Word of God community in Ann Arbor, Michigan, USA in 1969, were intended to tackle that problem. They were mainly designed to help *practising* Catholics who were sacramentalised but not fully evangelised by:

- Providing basic Christian teaching for the head.
- Helping people to come into a conscious awareness of God's unconditional mercy and love in their hearts.
- Assuring them that with new power in their hands, so to speak, their characters and lives could be transformed.

The seminars consist of seven meetings and talks. They can be divided into three groups:

- Seminars one to four prepare people for an in-filling of the Spirit.
  - Numbers one and two deal with the nature of salvation.
  - Number three is about the nature of the new life a person receives when he or she is filled with the Holy Spirit.
  - Number four describes how a person can prepare to receive the new life mentioned in the preceding seminar.
- The fifth seminar stands on its own. It is brief, practical and very important because it explains how each person will be prayed with for the in-filling of the Spirit, and any gift the Lord might want to bestow. The talk is followed by prayer ministry when people often come into a new awareness of the Lord. As theologian Fr. Peter Hocken has written, 'Baptism in the Spirit is a life transforming experience of the love of God the Father poured into one's heart by the Holy Spirit, received through a total surrender to the lordship of Jesus Christ.'

- Seminars six and seven are about Christian growth after the infilling of the Spirit.
  - The sixth seminar gives practical instruction about how to grow in the Spirit, for example, by means of daily prayer and scripture reading.
  - The seventh and last seminar is about the way in which people can put off their old nature with its worldly desires to put on their new nature in Christ. It also draws attention to predictable difficulties in the aftermath of baptism in the Spirit.

The Life in the Spirit Seminars are an inspired response to a pressing pastoral need. In an age of growing indifference to the Church, its teachings and disciplines they have helped millions of people to come into a deeper personal relationship with Jesus and to experience the infilling, guidance and charismatic gifts of the Holy Spirit. The Seminars, therefore, have proved to be one of the most effective means of renewal and evangelisation in the contemporary Church. On June 6th 2015 Vatican Radio carried a report of a two hour address of Pope Francis in the Latern Basilica to over 1,000 bishops and priests who attended an international clergy retreat. At one point he said, 'Speaking of dispensers of grace, I ask each and all of you that as part of the current of grace of Charismatic Renewal that you organise Life in the Spirit Seminars in your parishes and seminaries, schools, and neighborhoods, so as to share Baptism in the Spirit... It is a catechesis that produces, by the work of the Holy Spirit, a personal encounter with Jesus who changes lives.' Speaking to the members of Renewal in the Holy Spirit, at their

38th Italian National Convocation in Rome, on Fri. the 12th of July, 2015, Pope Francis said, 'work together with other Christians for the poor and the needy. We all have the same Baptism. Organise Life in the Spirit Seminars for brothers and sisters living on the street, and also for brothers and sisters marginalised by so much suffering in life.'

2. The Alpha Course
Alpha is the first letter in the Greek alphabet. The course teaches basic Christian truths. It is a ten-week introduction to the Christian faith that includes fifteen talks. They are available in Nicky Gumbel's book, *Alpha: Questions of Life* (Eastbourne: Kingsway, 2004). The topics covered include:

- 'Christianity; boring, untrue and irrelevant?'
- 'Who is Jesus?'
- 'Why did Jesus die?'
- 'Who is the Holy Spirit?'
- 'Why and how should I read the bible?'

It is important to stress the fact that the Alpha course is designed primarily to meet the needs of *unbelievers* and *lapsed* people. While it is true that the first Alpha course or two, will usually be attended by people who do practice their faith, the talks only become truly effective from an evangelistic point of view, if those first participants invite non-practising relatives, friends and colleagues to attend subsequent courses. The talks presume nothing and appeal to mind and heart. They try to persuade the listeners that what Christianity teaches is true without pressurising them in any way.

A typical session begins by welcoming the participants. Some groups start with a simple meal which is intended to build relationships and to foster a sense of belonging. Then there is a very brief time of prayer and hymn singing. Sometimes the leaders look at a few of the scripture texts that will be mentioned later in the talk. Then everyone listens either to the longer 40 min., or the shorter 20 min. version of the talk for that week which is given on DVD. Sometimes the talk is delivered live by a speaker who expresses in his or her own words the substance of what is in Nicky Gumbel's book *Alpha: Questions of Life*. There is a back up booklet that reminds participants of the key points. If there was no meal, then there is usually a 20 min break for biscuits tea and coffee. It is followed by a discussion in groups of five or six, each of which is facilitated by a member of the Alpha team. The evening ends at a predetermined time with a concluding prayer, such as the Our Father.

On week seven there is either a weekend or an extended day away. This enables people to deepen friendships, to hear a number of talks on the Holy Spirit, and also to receive prayer for an infilling of the Spirit. Following the Holy Spirit weekend or day, there are five more sessions.

Although Alpha started within an Anglican context, it has been accepted and approved at the highest level in the Catholic Church.

- In 2012 Rev. Nicky Gumbel, who has had such an influence on the growth of Alpha worldwide, was invited

to speak at the International Eucharistic Congress in Dublin.
- Bishop Michael Byrnes, auxiliary bishop for the Archdiocese of Detroit, was appointed as a member of the board of Alpha in the USA.
- Catholic representatives of Alpha in France were invited to attend the Synod of Bishops on the new evangelisation in Oct 2012.
- The Catholics in Alpha Ireland have received official approval from the Irish Conference of Bishops and relate to it by means of an officially appointed liaison person.

3. The Philip Course

Following a powerful calling from the Lord, Fr. Ricardo Argañaraz, an Argentinian, founded the John the Baptist Koinonia Community in Italy, in 1979. It is made up of priests, religious and about 3,500 lay members. It has spread to a number of countries in Europe, including Ireland.

The 'Philip Course' which was developed by the community is based on the Biblical story told in Acts 8:26-32 which describes the way one man's questions about faith were answered as a result of his providential encounter with Philip the evangelist.

Through a series of talks and spiritual exercises the Koinonia community take people on a three day journey of faith discovery. It follows the 6 points of the kerygma which we have already looked at in chapter eight. This course, like Alpha, is for non-believers and believers alike. It has helped to infuse thousands of people with a new, enthusiastic sense of Christian commitment.

Conclusion

There are many other evangelising courses which can be used, such as Cursillio, the Rite of Christian Initiation of Adults (RCIA), CaFE (Catholic Faith Exploration) etc. Although they have not been described in this chapter they are really worthwhile. It would have to be said that in Ireland the three we have described have proven to be the most successful as far as the new evangelisation is concerned.

Suggested questions for reflection and/or discussion

- Have you ever heard of any of these courses? If you have, did you attend any of them? How did that course help you to get closer to Jesus and to grow in faith?

- Some Catholics are critical of the courses mentioned in this chapter. They say that they are defective because they neglect to mention many important topics such as the sacraments, Our Lady, and the role of the Pope. What can be said to justify and defend the approach those courses take?

- What message and experience lies at the heart of these kerygmatic courses?

TWENTY SEVEN

NURTURING THE FAITH OF THE EVANGELISED

When people commit themselves to the Lord in a personal way as a result of such things as attending an Alpha course, Life in the Spirit Seminar, or person-to-person contact, the question arises, what happens next? Having been fully converted to Jesus, Christians have to grow to be his mature disciples. Remember what Jesus said in Mt 28:19, 'go and make *disciples* of all nations.' In the Greek N.T. a disciple is a pupil or apprentice who learns from someone more learned and experienced than he or she is. There are references to this notion in both the O.T. and the N.T.

A. In Sir 6:32-35 we read: 'If you wish, my son, you can be wise; if you apply yourself, you can be shrewd. If you are willing to listen, you can learn; if you pay attention, you can be instructed. Stand in the company of the elders; stay close to whoever is wise. Be eager to hear every discourse; let no insightful saying escape you. If you see the intelligent, seek them out; let your feet wear away their doorsteps!' It would seem that Jesus was a disciple in this sense when he was a boy of 12. We are told about how Joseph and Mary, 'After three days found him in the temple courts, sitting among the teachers, listening to them and asking them questions' (Lk 2:46) just as Sirach had advised.

B. In Mt 11:29 Jesus said: 'Learn from me, for I am gentle and humble of heart and you will find rest for your soul. For my yoke is easy and my burden is light.' As a young man Jesus was apprenticed to Joseph his father who was a carpenter. He would have learned from him how to carve yokes to fit oxen. Usually one side was for placement on a bigger, stronger, more experienced animal who would guide his smaller, weaker less experienced companion. Jesus is the master who teaches and guides his disciples. Committed members of the Christian community mediate Christ's pedagogic role by becoming companions and mentors who help new converts to mature in their relationship with the Lord and to express that intimacy in a loving way of living in our secular society. Sherry Weddell has written perceptively on this subject in her book, *Forming Intentional Disciples: The Path to Knowing and Following Jesus* (Huntington: Our Sunday Visitor, 2012) and in *Becoming a Parish of Intentional Disciples* (Huntington: Our Sunday Visitor, 2015). People become disciples in two main stages, namely, initial conversion and subsequent formation.

A. Conversion

As we saw earlier in the book conversion comes about as a result of having a personal encounter with Jesus. It could be the result of such things as talking to a friend who knows the Lord, hearing a powerful sermon, or attending an evangelisation course. They enable a person to pass from knowing about the person of Jesus to knowing him in person. This, however, is only the beginning of a new beginning.

B. Formation

A person becomes a full and mature disciple of Jesus not only as a result of receiving teaching about the doctrines and practices of the Christian life, but also by living in accord with those teachings and ethical guidelines. In par. 20 of his Apostolic Exhortation *Catechesis in Our Time*, Pope John Paul said, 'It is true that being a Christian means saying 'yes' to Jesus Christ, but let us remember that this 'yes' has two levels: It consists in surrendering to the word of God and relying on it, but it also means, at a later stage, endeavouring to know better - and better the profound meaning of this word.' The two interrelated stages of discipleship adverted to by St John Paul are mentioned in Heb 5:12-14, 'Although you should be teachers by this time, you need to have someone teach you again the basic elements of the utterances of God. You need milk, [and] not solid food. Everyone who lives on milk lacks experience of the word of righteousness, for he is a child. But solid food is for the mature, for those whose faculties are trained by practice to discern good and evil.' Speaking about the solid food of catechesis, Pope John Paul said in par. 21 of *Catechesis in our Time*,

- 'It must be systematic, not improvised but programmed to reach a precise goal;
- It must deal with essentials, without any claim to tackle all disputed questions or to transform itself into theological research or scientific exegesis;
- It must nevertheless be sufficiently complete, not stopping short at the initial proclamation of the Christian mystery such as we have in the kerygma;

- It must be an integral Christian initiation, open to all the other factors of Christian life.'

Many groups like the Charismatic Movement, Alpha and RCIA are good at bringing people to the point of knowing Jesus in person. But often they fail to nurture those who have been converted, by helping them to become mature, evangelising disciples of the Lord. Too often converted Catholics continue to focus on asking the question, what can Jesus do for me? rather than moving on to ask, what can I do for Jesus? Sherry Weddell has done a good deal of research on rates of discipleship among the 33% of American Catholics who still go to church on a regular basis. She discovered that of that 33% only 5% were disciples in the sense that they not only knew Jesus in a personal way, but had also committed their lives to him and were willing to do his will, no matter what sacrifices were involved, e.g. by avoiding premarital sex, not resorting to abortion, being honest in business etc. As Jesus said, 'If you hold to my teaching, you are really my disciples' (Jn 8:31-32). On another occasion Jesus added, 'As I have loved you, so you must love one another. By this all men will know that you are my disciples, if you love one another' (Jn 13:34-35).

Once Catholics have had a conversion experience these new disciples need three things:

- A sense of belonging (Returning to Church is recommended but it doesn't provide a sufficient sense of belonging)

- Good teaching (Hearing homilies on Sunday is good, but more systematic teaching is needed)
- Help in discovering and exercising their gifts. (While this can be done to a certain extent at parish level, it tends to focus on a select few rather than everyone)

If you look at parish websites you will see that they usually refer to as many as 40-50 groups. However, if they are examined in the light of the three points, just referred to, you will find that very few of them satisfy those three criteria. Parishes need groups like the following which help in the formation of committed disciples.

- Scripture study classes.
- *Lectio Divina* type of group prayer.
- Catechism Classes.
- Pastorates (Post Alpha groups).
- Parish Cells.
- The Legion of Mary.
- The Vincent de Paul Society.
- Charismatic prayer groups.

When people have been evangelised as a result of hearing and accepting the basic Christian teachings about Jesus, it would be really helpful if there was a card available which listed all the groups in the parish with a description of their purpose, when and where they meet, together with a list of contact people, phone numbers and email addresses. Here is a brief description of some groups that are really good at helping people to grow to be mature, committed disciples.

Bible Groups

Pope John Paul II said in par. 40 of *The Coming Third Millennium*, 'In order to recognise who Christ truly is, people should turn with renewed interest to the Bible, 'whether it be through the liturgy, rich in the divine word, or through devotional reading.' Pope Francis said in par. 175 of *The Joy of the Gospel*, 'The study of the sacred Scriptures must be a door opened to every believer It is essential that the revealed word radically enrich our catechesis and all our efforts to pass on the faith. Evangelisation demands familiarity with God's word, which calls for dioceses, parishes and Catholic associations to provide for a serious, ongoing study of the Bible, while encouraging its prayerful individual and communal reading.' One way of responding to advice of this kind would be to prayerfully reflect on the readings for the Mass of the coming Sunday. For instance, I know a parish which has a weekly 'Word on the Word' meeting. It lasts for one hour and consists of the following steps:

- A prayer for inspiration.
- One of the readings for the following Sunday's Mass is read by a participant.
- The participants prayerfully reflect on the text for about seven minutes. They are encouraged to address two questions, what was the inspired writer intending to say? How does his message relate to life today?
- The participants share in twos for about seven minutes by telling one another what came to them during their prayerful time of quiet reflection.
- Then the discussion is widened so that anyone can

share with the group. That can go on for up to twenty to twenty five minutes. It is fascinating to see how many complementary insights the participants can contribute. During this period of Bible sharing the person who is animating the session may offers exegetical and spiritual insights on the reading as a result of his or her Bible study before the meeting.
- The meeting ends with a prayer of thanksgiving. These meetings tend to attract a regular and appreciative clientele.

Those who attend comment on the fact that, not only are the meetings useful and edifying, they are a great preparation for hearing and understanding the liturgy of the word on the following Sunday.

Parish Cell Groups

In the mid 1980s, Dom Pigi Perini, of St. Estorgio parish in central Milan was looking for something that might revitalise his dying parish where only 5% of the people were practicing. He visited St. Boniface parish in Florida, and afterwards adopted and adapted the American version of the cell groups. Don Perini says that as a result of his visit to the U.S. he underwent a fundamental change of mentality. He moved from a maintenance model of parish to a missionary one, thereby taking to heart Paul VI's phrase that 'The Church exists to evangelise.' He introduced the cells into his parish in 1986. As a result, the structures and life of St. Eustorgio have been transformed over the last twenty five years. Currently there are around 120 groups with approximately ten people in each. They meet once a week. The group gatherings consist of seven key elements. Fr. Michael Hurley has written about them in, *Parish Cell Communities as Agents of Renewal in the Catholic Church in Ireland* (Lewiston: The Edwin Mellen Press, 2011). There is a Parish Cell website, *http://www.parishcellsireland.net/*

The seven purposes of Parish Evangelising Cells are spelled out as follows:

- To grow in an ongoing intimacy with the Lord.
- To share our Faith – evangelising by word and lifestyle.
- To grow in love of one another.
- To minister in the Body of Christ.
- To give and receive support.
- To raise up new leaders.
- To deepen our Catholic identity.

This is an outline of the timetable of cell meetings:
20 minutes: Prayer, song and scripture reflection. Each cell meeting begins with people quietly becoming aware of the presence of God. A few hymns or a spontaneous prayer greatly helps. There follows a reading and reflection upon scripture.
20 minutes: A review of prayer and evangelistic experiences since the previous meeting. Those who wish, briefly tell how they have seen the presence of God since they last met and of how they may have shared faith with another person.
10 minutes: A teaching on audio or videotape about some aspect of faith.

15-20 minutes: A discussion on the teaching, aimed at its understanding and application.
10-15 minutes: Intercessory and healing prayer.
Ending: A brief time of fellowship ends the meeting.

Pastorates

A number of years ago Alpha in England developed the notion of pastorates. Simply put, a pastorate is a small community of between 20-40 people within the larger community of the parish. Sometimes these larger groups contain a number of smaller groups. They function like an extended family or a small congregation. They grow spiritually together. They care for each other and serve one another. They also serve the larger community in different ways. Pastorates are communities in which a person can develop friendships, grow spiritually, develop spiritual gifts, help others grow, and impact the world — all in the context of caring, fun-filled relationships. I know that some parishes in Britain and Ireland have developed such groups and found that they are effective in helping newly evangelised people to grow to be mature disciples of the Lord.

Conclusion

Archbishop Martin of Dublin observed in an address, 'I believe that the transmission of the faith in the years to come will have to be more and more linked with the creation of faith communities, like the basic ecclesial communities that we speak about in the context of Africa or Latin America. These communities will help people, young and old, to be formed in their faith and to live it out concretely in a cultural context which is less and less supportive of faith. These communities must then, find their nourishment through their insertion into the broader communion of the Church in the common celebration of the Eucharist. *Our parishes must become communions of communities*, finding their unity again in the liturgy.'

All of those groups should have an evangelistic dimension. Before he ascended into heaven, Jesus gave this commission to his disciples, 'go and make disciples of all nations' (Mt 28:19). The two verbs used by Jesus are vital. Firstly, don't be a passive Christian, *go* out into the highways and byways of the world to evangelise. Secondly, the purpose of evangelisation is not just to bring people to faith in Christ but to *make* them full, committed disciples of the Lord. Jesus believed that the priority of evangelisation has to override other legitimate needs. As he said, 'Let the dead bury their dead. But you, go and proclaim the kingdom of God' (Lk 9:60). That is why par. 1816 of the *Catechism of the Catholic Church* says, 'The disciple of Christ must not only keep the faith and live on it; but also profess it, confidently bear witness to it, and spread it.'

SUGGESTED QUESTIONS FOR REFLECTION AND/OR DISCUSSION

• Would you agree that when people experience conversion to Jesus, perhaps as a result of attending an evangelisation course, it is not enough to merely urge them to attend church, parishes need to have smaller groups where their faith can be nurtured in a context of belonging?

• How many groups are there in your parish. Of those, how many involve such things as prayer, faith sharing and Christian teaching?

• Are any of the groups mentioned in this chapter operating in your parish? If not, do you think that one or more of them could be introduced as part of the structural change called for by Pope Francis?

Section Six:

Conclusion

TWENTY EIGHT

PRAYERFUL REFLECTION ON EVANGELISATION

Speaking to Asian bishops in 2014, Pope Francis warned against any form of apathetic evangelisation. He said, 'dialogue' and an 'openness to all' are essential in the Church's evangelisation. 'There can be no authentic dialogue,' he said, 'unless we are capable of opening our minds and hearts, in empathy and sincere receptivity, to those with whom we speak... We are challenged to listen not only to the words which others speak, but to the unspoken communication of their experiences, their hopes and aspirations, their struggles and their deepest concerns. Such empathy must be the fruit of our spiritual insight and personal experience, which lead us to see others as brothers and sisters, and to 'hear,' in and beyond their words and actions, what their hearts wish to communicate.' What the Pope said reminded me of some words of German theologian Dietrich Bonhoeffer in his book *Life Together* (New York: Harper & Row, 1978). He wrote, 'There is a kind of listening with half an ear that presumes already to know what the other person has to say. It is an impatient, inattentive listening... This is no fulfilment of our obligation, and it is certain that here too our attitude toward our brother only reflects our relationship to God... Christians have forgotten that the ministry of listening has been committed to them by Him who is Himself the great listener and whose work they should share. We should listen with the ears of God that we may speak the Word of God.' There is a story in the Old Testament that illustrates what the two men want evangelisers to avoid.

Apathetic listening

Job is the archetypal example of an afflicted person. As such he represents the needy people of our time, whether churchgoers or non churchgoers, who need to hear the Good News.. His story can teach evangelisers important lessons.

As you may recall, Job was a virtuous man, but he lost everything, his wife, family, livestock and possessions. As a result, he was not only afflicted in physical and emotional ways, he had to endure a spiritual crisis. The Jewish theology of his time maintained that misfortune like his was the result of personal sin. But Job knew that he had led a good life. So why was he suffering such adversity? He had no answer to this age-old question. As a result he felt bereft and even deserted by God.

Then three friends came to visit Job with the intention of bringing him good news. They sat silently observing him for a long time. They were aware of his suffering. But they failed to pay attention to him in an empathic way. Theirs was a more detached and objective form of relationship. The three men sensed that if they attended, in an open-minded way, to Job's sufferings and their implications, they would have to face a religious dilemma. They would have to let go of their current understanding of good and evil, without necessarily being able to replace it with a new one. In the event they were more concerned with theological orthodoxy, and the sense of personal security it gave them, than they were with the disquieting challenge posed by Job's situation. Clearly, they trusted more in the religion of God than they did in the God of religion. They argued that, although he seemed to be a good man, they presupposed that Job *must* have offended God is some secret way. How else could his plight be explained. So in the name of a religious truth, they denied the truth of Job's lived experience.

The Lord responded to the three men by telling them that instead of being displeased with the weeping, mourning and complaints of Job, he was displeased with them. They were like the priest in the parable of the Good Samaritan. Although they were aware of Job's suffering, they avoided any real involvement with him. Lacking in genuine empathy they focused, in an apathetic way, on theological formulae rather than on Job's problematic feelings. They kept him, and the thorny issues raised by his sufferings, at arm's length, by resorting to pious cliches .

Instead of comforting Job, the trio's lack of empathic understanding increased his sense of anguish and isolation. Job responded to his friends by saying: 'I have understanding as well as you' (Job 12:3). And again: 'I have heard many such things....I also could speak as you do, if you were in my place; I could join words together against you, and shake my head at you. I could strengthen you with my mouth, and the solace of my lips would assuage your pain' (Job 16,2; 4-5). And again, echoing the sentiments of many misunderstood people down the centuries, Job said: 'Oh that you would keep silent, and it would be your wisdom!' (Job 13: 5).

PRAXIS AND THEOLOGICAL REFLECTION

Arguably there are two kinds of theology. Firstly, there is the academic, bookish kind which the three friends espoused. Secondly, there is a practical kind which is the result of reflection on lived experience like Job's. This second approach is sometimes referred to as praxis theology. Pope Francis has written about it in pars 231-232 of *The Joy of the Gospel*. He states, 'There exists a constant tension between ideas and realities. Realities simply are, whereas ideas are worked out. There has to be continuous dialogue between the two, lest ideas become detached from realities. It is dangerous to dwell in the realm of words alone... Ideas – conceptual elaborations – are at the service of communication, understanding, and praxis.' The notion of Christian praxis is a relatively new one and associated with the liberation theology of South America. It refers to the continual interplay between one's experience of evangelisation and ideas about such evangelisation. Prayerful reflection on that interplay will lead to insights that will enrich one's future efforts at evangelising.

The kind of prayerful reflection the Pope has in mind is sometimes referred to as theological reflection. Bishop Laurie Green says in his book, *Let's Do Theology: Resources for Contextual Theology* (New York: Bloomsbury/Mowbray, 2009) that, 'Theological reflection is thus: bringing into juxtaposition our present life experience [e.g., that of evangelising] and the treasures of our Christian heritage [e.g., Biblical and contemporary Church texts], to check one against the other, to let each talk to the other, to learn from the mix and to gain even more insight to add to the store of Christian heritage.' The best way to bring one's experience of evangelising into dialogue with our Christian heritage, is to reflect in a prayerful way upon them both.

Reflection on one's evangelisation

Whenever we have been evangelising, e.g., in a person-to-person way, or in a more collective context such as running an Alpha Course, it is good to reflect upon what has happened, during a quiet time. It might be useful to ask oneself questions like the following:

- Who talked the most, you or the person you wanted to evangelise? When you listened, did you do so with empathy by seeking to sense and understand what the other person was sharing?
- Did you get round to talking about Jesus Christ, or were you content with a more general discussion about religious and spiritual topics?
- Did fear or human respect prevent you from evangelising in an un-self-conscious way?
- Did you identify any stepping stone to faith in the course of listening to the person? Did you take the opportunity presented by the stepping stone in order to discuss meaning of life issues?

- What feelings were evoked within you as you evangelised? Were they positive, such as admiration, liking, satisfaction etc? Or were they negative, such as irritation, impatience, anxiety etc? What *perceptions* evoked those feelings? It is worth remembering that we don't have feelings about external events, but about our perceptions of them, coloured as they are by so many subjective factors such as our assumptions, prejudices, values, attitudes, beliefs or personal memories.
- Did the person you were trying to evangelise raise any issues that made you feel uncomfortable, e.g., why the innocent suffer; why God often seems to fail to answer petitionary and intercessory prayers; why there is so much sex abuse in the Church?
- At any point did you take the opportunity to briefly share your own faith story?
- While you listened with one ear to the person you hoped to evangelise, did you listen with the other to the inspirations of the Lord?
- Did any opportunity arise when it was appropriate for you to share a relevant scripture text with the person?
- Did you conclude the dialogue by offering to pray with the person for some special intention? How did it go?
- Did the person you were evangelising ask you a question you couldn't answer? How did you respond?

The importance of prayer

Having reflected in the way suggested, it is important to share your reactions, thoughts and desires with the Lord. Having done so, it is even more important to spend a quiet time in the presence of the Lord, listening to anything that the Father or the Son might want to say to you, e.g., in and through a scripture text, an inner prompting, voice, image, or vision. In other words, not only do we grow in evangelistic self-awareness as we pray in the presence of the Lord, we receive all kinds of insights. They enable us to make resolutions which are single, precise and possible which will enable us to evangelise more effectively in the future than we did in the past. Furthermore this kind of prayerful reflection will often raise questions which can only be answered by asking for advice or reading relevant articles or books.

Conclusion

There is a quotation which is attributed to Socrates (469–99 B.C.) which says that, 'The unexamined life is not worth living.' As evangelisers we will keep growing in theological insight and practical skill if we reflect on our experiences of success and failure in a prayerful way. As Frank Duff once said, 'failure is just another word for postponed success,' and C.S. Lewis said in like manner, 'Failures, repeated failures, are finger posts on the road to achievement. One fails forward toward success.'

Suggested questions for reflection and or discussion

- Did you ever have a Job like experience where people who were well intentioned failed to listen to you in an empathic way? Have you ever treated another person in an equally insensitive way when you were engaged in evangelisation?

- Would you agree that if we don't learn from our mistakes we are likely to repeat them?

- When you engage in evangelisation of one kind or another do you reflect prayerfully about it afterwards?

TWENTY NINE

SOME OBSTACLES TO EVANGELISATION

In this more lengthy chapter I would like to draw attention to some impediments to the new evangelisation. The list is not intended to be in any way exhaustive. The topics are not listed in order of importance. We will look briefly at six of them:

- Lack of poverty of spirit
- Universalism
- Relativism
- Scandal
- Loss of a sense of sin
- The Role of the Evil One

1. Lack of poverty of spirit
Jesus said that he came to bring the good news to the poor, i.e. those who are aware of their need and desire for God. In other words, there is no blessing or growth in the Christian life without preceding desire. The deeper and stronger the desire for God and God's blessings the greater the openness to the presence, word and will of God. In our culture many people fail to acknowledge that sense of need for two main reasons.

Firstly, they have become preoccupied with, and reliant upon worldly things such as money, possessions, security, reputation, status, influence and pleasure. Years ago I heard a preacher quote some words of Jesus from Mt 6:21, 'where your treasure is, there your heart will be also.' Then he said, 'whatever you think about most is your treasure.' Often it is one or more of the worldly things already mentioned. In effect they becomes idols, substitutes for God.

Secondly, many people in our media soaked culture are overly extroverted and consequently have become alienated from their own deepest selves and desires. As Pope Paul VI once wrote, 'Today our psychology is turned outward too much. The exterior scene is so absorbing that our attention is mainly directed outside; we are nearly always absent from our innermost being.' A certain hubris can be the result. There are many people in our culture, who in the words of T. S. Eliot in his *Four Quartets*, are 'are distracted from distraction by distraction,' and have little or no sense of needing God. In their view, if God does exist, the deity is distant and silent. But as Pope John Paul II said in his book *Crossing the Threshold of Hope*, 'It is truly difficult to speak of the silence of God. We must speak, rather, of the *desire to stifle the voice of God.*' Surely that is true. As Jesus observed, 'In them is fulfilled the prophecy of Isaiah: 'You will be ever hearing but never understanding; you will be ever seeing but never perceiving. For this people's heart has become calloused; they hardly hear with their ears, and they have closed their eyes. Otherwise they might see with their eyes, hear with their ears, understand with their hearts and turn' (Mt 13:14-15).

If people refuse to listen to the Good News, it is better to wipe the dust off your shoes, as Jesus suggested in Lk 9:5, and to go to those who are aware of their need for something beyond themselves, and who identify with the words of a U2 song, 'I still have not found what I'm looking for.'

2. Universalism

The scriptures give the impression that perhaps only a minority of people will be saved. Here are a few examples:

- In Mt 7:13-14 Jesus said, 'Enter through the narrow gate. For wide is the gate and broad is the road that leads to destruction, and many enter through it. But small is the gate and narrow the road that leads to life, and only a few find it.'
- In Mt 22:14 he added, 'For many are invited, but few are chosen.'
- St. Peter stated that, 'It is difficult for good people to be saved; what, then, will become of godless sinners?' (1 Pt 4:18).

In spite of these scripture texts, many of our contemporaries believe that the road that leads to heaven is wide and that most people take it, with the possible exception of some extraordinarily evil people. Many priests seem to agree with this point of view and so in their preaching they avoid mentioning the possibility of forfeiting salvation and having to endure eternal separation from God. The late Cardinal Avery Dulles wrote, 'The mass for the dead has turned into a Mass of the

Resurrection, which sometimes seems to celebrate not so much the resurrection of the Lord as the salvation of the deceased, without any reference to sin and punishment. More education is needed to convince people that they ought to fear God, who as Jesus taught, can punish soul and body together in hell (cf. Mt 10:28).' As Pope John Paul II pointed out, some preachers, 'no longer have the courage to preach the threat of hell. And perhaps even those who listen to them have stopped being afraid of hell.'

For example a few years ago a very well-known Irish broadcaster died suddenly. It emerged after his death that although he earned a half million euro each year he was very much in debt. Apparently he had led an opulent life style, and had been a drug addict all his adult life. It resulted in the break up of his marriage. Having left his wife and children he lived with a divorced woman. It was clear that, in spite of his good points, he had feet of clay like the rest of us. However, a well-known priest said on the radio that the deceased was a remarkably good man, so much so that he was quite sure he was in heaven. Then he added, 'and if he is not in heaven I have no desire to go there myself.' In other words, although the deceased had many obvious, public faults the priest had canonised him, thereby saying in effect, there was no need to pray that God might have mercy on his soul. If people think that we are saved no matter what we believe or how we behave, it is not surprising that evangelisation, and the demands of Christian discipleship don't make much impression.

3. Relativism

Secular culture is said to be *postmodern* in nature. This world view maintains that, rather than being an objective fact, our knowledge of truth is subjective and at best probable, partial and provisional. Pope John Paul II described it in par. 91 of *Faith & Reason* in these words, 'the currents of thought which claim to be postmodern merit appropriate attention. According to some of them, the time of certainties is irrevocably past, and the human being must now learn to live in a horizon of total absence of meaning, where everything is provisional and ephemeral.' Postmodernist relativism poses a very real challenge as far as evangelisation is concerned.

Christians believe that God has revealed absolute truth in and through the person and teachings of Jesus Christ and that he is the sole mediator between God and human beings (cf. 1 Tim 2:5). There is no other name by which people can be saved (cf. Acts 4:12). However, people in postmodern culture find those claims very hard to accept. They tend to see Jesus as merely one outstanding religious leader among many others such as Buddha, Lau Tzu, Zoroaster and Mohammed. Any claim that Christ is unique and the sole means of salvation is considered to be arrogant, intolerant and unjustified. They consider all religions as equally valid paths to transcendence.

Pope Emeritus Benedict XVI said on Oct 23rd 2014, 'Many today think religions should respect each other and, in their dialogue, become a common force for peace. According to this way of thinking, it is usually taken for granted that different religions are variants of one and the same reality. The question of truth, that which originally motivated Christians more than any other, is here put inside parentheses. It is assumed that the authentic truth about God is in the last analysis unreachable and that at best one can represent the ineffable with a variety of symbols. This renunciation of truth seems realistic and useful for peace among religions in the world. It is nevertheless lethal to faith.'

While many people in Western countries have parted company with institutional forms of religion they will often say that they are spiritual. That phrase covers a multitude. Usually it refers to an arbitrary *potpurri* of beliefs drawn from different religions, psychology and the occult. Because of the current spirit of the age, people like this often reject the Christian claim that Christ and his message are manifestations of absolute, revealed truth. So they often resist the claims of Christian evangelisers.

4. Scandal
Jesus said on one occasion, 'your light must shine before others, that they may see your good deeds and glorify your heavenly Father.' The Popes have said much the same in their documents on evangelisation. For example in par. 42 of *Mission of the Redeemer,* Pope John Paul said, 'People today, put more trust in witnesses than in teachers, in experience than in teaching, and in life and action than in theories. The witness of a Christian life is the first and irreplaceable form of mission: Christ, whose mission we continue, is the 'witness' *par excellence* (Rev 1:5; 3:14) and the model of all Christian witness.'

The problem with the Church is that many of its members do not practice what they preach. There is nothing new about this. For example, in the *Second Letter of Clement* (A.D. 100 approx.) the anonymous author said that it was not too surprising that the name of the Lord was blasphemed by the pagans. 'For when the pagans hear from our mouths the words of God, they marvel at their beauty and greatness. But when they discover that our actions are not worthy of the words we speak, they turn from wonder to blasphemy, saying that it is a myth and a delusion. For when they hear from us that God says, 'It is no credit to you if you love those who love you, but it is a credit to you if you love your enemies and those who hate you,' when they hear these things, they marvel at such extraordinary goodness. But, when they see that we do not only fail to love those who hate us we even fail to love those who love us, they scornfully laugh at us, and the Name is blasphemed.'

Is it any different nowadays? Divisions in and between the churches rob the Gospel message of its credibility. As Pope Francis has observed in par of *The Joy of the Gospel*, 'The credibility of the Christian message would be much greater if Christians could overcome their divisions and the Church could realise the fullness of catholicity proper to her.' Another cause of scandal, in a number of countries, is the vile phenomenon of child sex abuse by priests and religious. It is clear in Ireland that the virtual collapse of the Church's influence, together with a big decline in church attendance, and lack of priestly vocations has coincided with those scandals. Is it any wonder that many nominal Christians think that, instead of being a way of salvation Catholicism is a sickness that mistakes itself for a cure.

5. Loss of a Sense of Sin

Explicit or implicit awareness of sin is a prerequisite for openness to the message of salvation in Christ because Christ died for the forgiveness of sins. But as Pope Pius XII famously observed in the mid 20th century, 'the sin of the century is the loss of a sense of sin.'

Pope John Paul II provided an insightful answer to the question, why are so many people unaware of their wrongdoing in par. 18 of his Apostolic Exhortation *Reconciliation & Confession* which contained a section entitled, 'The Loss of a Sense of Sin.' Pope Benedict XVI has observed, 'the word 'sin' is not accepted by many, for it pre-supposes a religious vision of the world and of man. If we eliminate God from the horizon of the world, we cannot speak of sin. Just as when the sun is hidden the shadows disappear and the shadows appear only if the sun is there, so too the eclipse of God necessarily brings the eclipse of sin.' The core Christian message is about God's willingness to forgive sin, in virtue of Christ's saving death on the cross. But often, due to a lack of a sense of sin, people fail to see the relevance of the Christian message. They have little or no sense that they need to be saved from their own guilt.

6. The Role of the Evil One

The New Testament says that one reason that evangelisation is not always successful is the malign role of the devil.

- In the parable of the Sower Jesus said in, 'When anyone hears the message about the kingdom and does not

understand it, the evil one comes and snatches away what was sown in his heart' (Mt 13:18-23)
- In 2 Cor 4:4 St. Paul said something very similar, 'The god of this age [i.e. Satan] has blinded the minds of unbelievers, so that they cannot see the light of the gospel of the glory of Christ, who is the image of God.' It is clear from these scripture texts that the devil can prevent worldly people from hearing the life-giving word of God.

Arguably, the devil has a hand in the four obstacles already mentioned.

However it is important to remember that in Jn 12:31 Jesus said, 'now shall the *ruler of this world* be cast out.' Ever since His saving death and resurrection, that is already true in *principle* But how can Satan's power be overcome in *practice*?

As far as the evangelising person is concerned he or she intercedes with confidence for himself and others, believing as St. Paul said, 'For though we live in the world, we do not wage war as the world does. The weapons we fight with are not the weapons of the world. On the contrary, they have divine power to demolish strongholds [of Satan in the mind]. We demolish arguments and every pretension that sets itself up against the knowledge of God, and we take captive every thought to make it obedient to Christ' (2 Cor 10:4-5).

Those who are familiar with the ministry of intercession appreciate the fact that it takes place within a context of spiritual conflict. As St. Paul once warned: 'For our struggle is not against flesh and blood, but against the rulers, against the authorities, against the powers of this dark world and against the spiritual forces of evil in the heavenly realms' (Eph 6:12). Sometimes we have to pray for people, such as relatives, friends and acquaintances that they may be freed from the spiritual oppression that currently prevents them from hearing and understanding the word of God. As we saw in chapter fourteen, the New Springtime Community says in its mission statement, We will 'encourage intercessors to pray on our behalf that we may be delivered from all evil and empowered to proclaim the Good News effectively.'

SUGGESTED QUESTIONS FOR REFLECTION AND/OR DISCUSSION

- In your opinion which of the obstacles mentioned in this chapter is the most formidable obstacle where evangelisation is concerned? Why so?

- If you were asked to mention an extra obstacle, what would it be?

- When you are confronted with obstacles in your life, how do you cope with them, from a spiritual point of view?

THIRTY

THE COURAGE TO EVANGELISE: SOME PERSONAL REFLECTIONS

The prospect of engaging in evangelisation of any kind can be intimidating. Some people are naturally shy, and they may feel that they don't have the skill to initiate conversations on religious topics. Because others feel that religion is a private matter, they suspect that it would be too intrusive to talk about faith issues. Frank Duff, founder of The Legion of Mary, spoke about this phenomenon in *The Legion Handbook*. He said that many would-be evangelisers are scared by the prospect 'of a few jeers, or angry words, or criticism, or even amused looks, or from a fear that he or she may be thought to be preaching or making an affectation of holiness... This timidity, is commonly called human respect, ...For different people the latter assumes different labels: 'common prudence,' 'respect for the opinion of others,' 'hopelessness of the enterprise,' 'waiting for a lead,' and many other plausible phrases, all of which lead to inaction.'

When we read the New Testament we find that there is nothing new in this situation. The first disciples were crippled by fear until they received the outpouring of the Holy Spirit at Pentecost. Sometime later, when the believers met with persecution and the possibility of martyrdom they again felt afraid. They prayed, 'Enable your servants to speak your word *with great boldness*' (Acts 4:29). Then we are told that, 'After they prayed, the place where they were meeting was shaken. And they were all filled with the Holy Spirit and spoke the word of God boldly' (Acts 4:31). In Eph 6:20 Paul said, 'Pray that I may declare it fearlessly, as I should.' In 2 Tim 1:7-8 Paul said to Timothy, his protégé, 'God did not give us a spirit of timidity, but a spirit of power, of love and of self-discipline. So do not be ashamed to testify about our Lord.' Pope Francis echoed those sentiments when he wrote in par. 259 of *The Joy of the Gospel,* 'The Holy Spirit also grants the courage to proclaim the newness of the Gospel with boldness (*parrhesía*) in every time and place, even when it meets with opposition.'

I'd have to admit that in the past anxiety, fear and human respect have prevented me doing many things including evangelisation. As I wrestled with this issue in prayer, I discovered a way of mastering my fears in order to act with courage. I would like to recount three interrelated experiences.

A Personal Word

In the early 1980s I lived in Boston, USA. I have explained in *Guided by God* (Luton: New Life, 2015) that while I was there I experienced an extended period of desolation of spirit. On one occasion I went to a Jesuit retreat centre in Weston, Massachusetts, to attend a directed retreat. It didn't go well and I felt very disheartened. One evening as I lay on my bed I tried to pray. Suddenly, an image came into my mind. I could see a dimly lit cave. There was a rock in the middle upon which rested an open book. Immediately I thought to myself, 'that's the Bible, if I read what it says on its open pages, God will speak to me.' But when I approached the book, I was disappointed and frustrated to find that its pages were blank! I can remember saying to the Lord, 'Why do you refuse to speak to me in this darkness?' A few minutes later I thought I heard an inner voice saying to me, 'I will speak to you. Read Is 41:10.' At first I was sceptical, feeling that this was a false inspiration, an example of wishful thinking on my part. However, I opened the Bible and read these words, 'fear not, for I am with you, be not dismayed, for I am your God; I will strengthen you, I will help you, I will uphold you with my victorious right hand.' Those words of the Lord really ministered to me. They were so relevant at the time. While they didn't console me in an emotional sense, they gave me the strength to keep going. As Ps 23:4 puts it, 'Even though I walk through the valley of the shadow of death, I will fear no evil, for you are with me; your rod and your staff [the words and Spirit of God], they comfort me.'

In 1987 I had a related experience when I travelled to Italy to speak at a conference in Assisi. When I got to Rome I was like a wound-up spring, full of stress. The prospect of having to cope with the language, currency, travel, and the talks filled me with apprehension and dread. I remember praying to God for help. In spite of my many petitions nothing seemed to happen. I can recall that, at one point I felt an inner voice was saying, 'cut the scriptures at random and I will speak to you.' Typically, I doubted that this was a genuine inspiration. But eventually I said 'O.K.', uttered a prayer for guidance, closed my eyes, opened the bible, and put my finger on the page. When I read the verse I was pointing at, I discovered that it was Is 41:10, 'fear not, for I am with you, be not dismayed, for I am your God; I will strengthen you, I will help you, I will uphold you with my victorious right hand.' It was the very same one I had read in Boston years before! I said to the Lord, 'Thanks, that verse is relevant once again, and means a lot to me. Now, please take away my fear.' Nothing happened. Having voiced my feelings of let-down and anger to the Lord, I took another look at the verse. It began, 'Fear not.' Suddenly, I realised that, rather than being a word of advice, it was in fact a word of command. So in obedience to God's word I summoned up all my reserves of courage and said, 'O.K. Lord, I will not be afraid, I will take on the whole of Italy if necessary, but I can't do it on my own, you will have to help me.' As soon as I uttered those heartfelt words, a great calm came over me. Tension left my body as I realised that, with God's help, I would be well able to cope. And so I did. When I got to Assisi my ministry was richly blessed in a number of ways.

In November 2014 I conducted a mission in Billings, Montana. My last Sunday there was the feast of Christ the King. During mass I preached a challenging, but overly severe, homily which asked, who sits on the throne, you or the Lord? When I came back to Ireland I received a very critical email from someone who hated my homily and which was full of judgement and condemnation from beginning to end. Although, I felt that the sentiments in the email were not inspired by the Holy Spirit, the accusations it contained got under my skin and played upon my mind. In December I went away for a five day retreat in a Benedictine monastery. I prayed a lot about the email. I fervently asked the Lord to speak a liberating word to my heart. Towards the end of the retreat I bought a book by Jack Deere, entitled *Surprised by the Voice of God* (Grand Rapids: Zondervan, 1996) from the library to my room. At one point I opened it at random and came across an inspiring story about a woman who suffered a complete mental breakdown. She was sent to a mental institution where she languished for many years. Her mind was full of negative thoughts, e.g., that she had sinned against the Holy Spirit and as a result was completely and forever cut off from God. A man called Paul Cain got a prophetic word that he should visit this woman and pray for her and heal her. He did what God prompted him to do. He did pray for the woman and she experienced the liberating power of the Lord. Paul Cain said to her, 'When I leave here, the madness is going to try to return. God is going to put a scripture in your heart when I walk out this door. That scripture is going to seal your healing.' Soon after he left, the woman recalled, Is 41:10. When she heard the evil voice whisper to her she said, it is written, 'fear not, for I am with you, be not dismayed, for I am your God; I will strengthen you, I will help you, I will uphold you with my victorious right hand.' The icy hand let go, the voice became silent. Three days later she left the hospital never to return. As soon as I read those words, tears streamed down my face. I was certain that God the Father was speaking to me. I knew that instead of listening to my feelings I should put all my trust in God's word. As I put my faith in what God had said, all the oppression I had been feeling lifted from me and it hasn't returned.

REFLECTION ON IS 41:10

Fear of evangelising is natural and understandable. However, while we acknowledge our fears, we should act in accordance with the word and will of God. Is 41:10 begins with the words 'Fear not,' They are not words of advice but a word of divine instruction. So in obedience to God the evangeliser has to make an act of will, 'in spite of my fears I will be courageous with the help of God.' The Lord assures evangelisers that 'I Am with you,' 'I am your God.' This is a very evocative assurance. When Moses asked God who he was, he replied, 'I am who Am' (Ex 3:14). There is a New Testament echo of that sentiment in John's Gospel where Jesus makes a number of 'I am' statements, e.g. 'I am the bread of life,' 'I am the light of the world,' 'I am the gate for the sheep,' 'I am the good shepherd,' 'I am the way and the truth and the life,' 'I am the true vine.' When he was asked if he was the king of the Jews, Jesus answered, 'You are right in saying I AM a king' (Jn 18:37). The deity is described as 'I am,' the One who is with us in the person of Jesus who is our God.

The Lord makes three infallible promises in Is 41:10:

- 'I will strengthen you.' This verse reminds me of a number of St Paul's paradoxical statements, such as, 'My grace is sufficient for you, for my power is made perfect in weakness. Therefore I will boast all the more gladly about my weaknesses, so that Christ's power may rest on me.' (2 Cor 12:9), In Phil 4:13 he says, 'I can do all things through Christ who strengthens me.'
- 'I will help you.' This promise remind me of Hebrews

13: 5-6 which reads, 'God has said, 'Never will I leave you; never will I forsake you.' So we say with confidence, 'The Lord is my helper; *I will not be afraid*. What can man do to me?'
- 'I will uphold you with my victorious right hand.' I like the word 'victory here.' The Lord who is the victor will uphold us as we evangelise. In 2 Chron 20:15 we read, 'the battle is not yours, but God's,' and in Zech 4:6, "Not by might nor by power, but by my Spirit,' says the Lord Almighty.'

CONCLUSION

Many, many years ago, I came across the following quotation from Winston Churchill, 'Courage is rightly esteemed the first of human qualities... because it is the quality which guarantees all others.' Surely, there is a lot of truth in what he says. We need courage to face all the challenges of everyday life. It is no different when it comes to the challenges presented by the call to evangelise. The Spirit we have received is not a spirit of timidity or fear, but rather one of courageous self-control (cf. 2 Tim 1:7).

Suggested questions for reflection and/or discussion

- What scares you most about your call to share your faith with others?

- What form of evangelising do you find most intimidating?

- How do you overcome your fear and act with a spirit of courage and boldness?

Further copies of this book can be obtained from

Goodnews Books
Upper level
St. John's Church Complex
296 Sundon Park Road
Luton, Beds. LU3 3AL

www.goodnewsbooks.co.uk
orders@goodnewsbooks.co.uk
01582 571011

other books by
by Pat Collins C.M.
also available

Prophecy
Guided by God
He Has Anointed Me
Basic Evangelisation
Gifted and Sent
Mind and Spirit
Word and Spirit
The Gifts of the Spirit and the New Evangelisation